PERSONAL RELATIONSHIPS:
Their Structures and Processes

JOHN M. MacEACHRAN MEMORIAL
LECTURE SERIES,

Sponsored by
The Department of Psychology
The University of Alberta
with the support of
The Alma Mater Fund of the University of Alberta
in memory of John M. MacEachran,
pioneer in Canadian psychology

PERSONAL RELATIONSHIPS:
Their Structures and Processes

HAROLD H. KELLEY
University of California, Los Angeles

 LAWRENCE ERLBAUM ASSOCIATES, PUBLISHERS
1979   Hillsdale, New Jersey

DISTRIBUTED BY THE HALSTED PRESS DIVISION OF

JOHN WILEY & SONS

New York   Toronto   London   Sydney

Lawrence Erlbaum Associates, Inc., Publishers
62 Maria Drive
Hillsdale, New Jersey 07642

Distributed solely by Halsted Press Division
John Wiley & Sons, Inc., New York

Library of Congress Cataloging in Publication Data

Kelley, Harold H.
  Personal relationships

  (John M. MacEachran memorial lecture series; 1978)
  Bibliography: p.
  Includes index.
  1. Interpersonal relations.   I. Title.   II. Series.
HM132.K44   301.11   79-11609
ISBN 0-470-26730-5

Printed in the United States of America

Contents

Foreword

The vigor and intellectual development of social psychology emanated from the genius of a group of social psychologists working at Kurt Lewin's Research Center for Group Dynamics at the Massachusetts Institute of Technology. These social psychologists initiated work on communication processes, social motivation and person perception. We are very honored to have Harold Kelley, a member of this group, as our fourth MacEachran lecturer. As I shall chronicle events, you'll see that many of the major developments in the field of social psychology have been marked by the presence of Harold Kelley.

His intial work in psychology began with his study of measurement, statistics, social, physiological and experimental psychology at the University of California at Berkeley. After obtaining his master of arts degree there, he was associated with the Aviation Psychology Program of the Army Air Force during the war. Based on his association with Stuart Cook and others, his interest in social psychology developed into a career decision. Advised by Cook, and encouraged by his association with a number of other aspiring social psychologists, he went to Lewin's Research Center for Group Dynamics at the Massachusetts Institute of Technology in 1946. During this time he did his research on first impressions in interpersonal relations under the advice of Dorwin Cartwright. After obtaining his doctoral degree, he went to the University of Michigan where he worked with Leon Festinger, engaging in studies of social attitudes and informal social communication within communities and in small groups. He then joined the faculty at Yale University and was part of the group conducting research on attitude change, persuasive communication and attitude scaling with Irving Janis and Carl Hovland. In this program they developed a major systematic approach to the psychological processes underlying communication and attitude change.

He continued his studies of social power, influence and communication at the University of Minnesota, and in 1957, at the Center for Advanced Study in the Behavioral Sciences, developed a collaborative relationship with John Thibaut that eventuated in the publication of a book *The Social Psychology of Groups*. This book, which presented a systematic theory of group processes and stimulated much research on bargaining, negotiation, and coalition formation, has become identified as one of the several major contributions to an exchange theory perspective on social behavior.

His position in 1961 at the University of California, Los Angeles has continued to the present and in that time he has not only completed further research on the social psychology of groups, bargaining and conflict but has developed theoretical work in the area of causal attribution. In this approach, concerned with the development of causal inferences about behavior, he returned to his historical origins in gestalt theory. His ideas have provided an impetus for research and have melded with those of others to spark new ideas that have enriched theoretical developments and opened new empirical areas. While there is no doubt that his work on the social psychology of groups has been influential, it is very clear that his work on attribution theory has had an impact on the field to a greater extent perhaps than that of any recent theorist in the area of social psychology.

During his career he has, of course, been functioning as a member of many editorial boards and consulting editorships of our major journals; he has been President of Division 8 of the American Psychological Association, President of the Western Psychological Association, and has served other professional functions too numerous to detail here.

Recognition of his considerable contribution to the field of psychology was formalized by his being awarded the Distinguished Scientific Contribution Award in 1971 from the American Psychological Association. I quote his citation, "For the development of fundamental theory that has given a systematic framework to research on interpersonal processes and for penetrating and insightful experimental studies that have illuminated and extended our understanding of these processes".

His current endeavors include theoretical work on conjuring, the art of attribution manipulation and magic, and on close relationships. The material presented herein represents what Hal Kelley has thought and learned about the social psychology of close relationships.

Brendan Gail Rule
University of Alberta

Preface

It is an honor to contribute to the succession of distinguished books based on the MacEachran Memorial Lecture Series, sponsored by the Department of Psychology at the University of Alberta. I gave the fourth lectures in this series on March 27 to 29, 1978, and have spent the four months since preparing them for this book. When invited to give the lectures, I decided to combine a description of my own recent research on young couples with a proposal for a theoretical framework for viewing such relationships. In the execution the second purpose has become the dominant one. My research has proven to be suggestive of some of the necessary key concepts in the theoretical analysis. However, the research was not done with this total framework in mind, so it cannot be considered in any sense a "test" of the concepts.

With regard to the theoretical analysis, the reader will realize that this is a progress report—an account of ideas that are still in the progress of development. I am confident that the starting point of the analysis is a good one. The ideas take account of what are certainly the central phenomena of the personal relationship. I also have a good deal of confidence in the long-term viability of the types of concepts adopted for analyzing these phenomena. I am less sure of the particular ways the concepts are specified and ordered here. They serve to organize and give meaning to a diverse array of interpersonal events, but their derivations and operationalizations are not as clear at this time as I would like.

I am deeply grateful to the psychologists at the University of Alberta for providing the opportunity and the impetus to assemble these data and develop these ideas. I will long appreciate the hospitality extended me, by faculty and students alike, during my stay in Edmonton. Special thanks are due Eugene Lechelt for his excellent arrangements and Brendan and Stanley Rule for their kind attentions.

The final manuscript had the benefit of comments by Janusz Grzelak, George Levinger, John Thibaut, and Scott Wimer, to each of whom I am very grateful. My intellectual debt to John Thibaut extends far beyond his comments on this particular manuscript. As will be evident from frequent references to our co-authored works, most of the basic ideas in this book have been developed by us jointly in the many discussions associated with our several writing projects.

The research of my colleagues and myself reported in this book was supported by grants from the National Science Foundation (GS-33069X and BNS-76-20490).

H. H. Kelley

PERSONAL RELATIONSHIPS:
Their Structures and Processes

Introduction 1

This book summarizes certain concepts and evidence regarding the nature of close personal relationships. Its purpose is to suggest how such relationships are to be conceptualized for scientific analysis. What are the essential properties of a personal relationship? What are its necessary defining structures and processes?

In everyday usage, we use the term *close personal relationship* to refer to lovers, marriage partners, best friends, and persons who work closely together. An everyday description of this kind of relationship will refer to its long-lasting nature; the fact that the persons spend much time together, do many things together, and (often) share living or working quarters; the intercommunication of personal information and feelings; and the likelihood that the persons see themselves as a unit and are seen that way by others.

In this book I attempt to formulate a scientific description to take the place of this everyday one. The purpose is to gain an understanding of such relationships that will make possible their systematic assessment and classification and provide a basis for interventions to improve their functioning. The underlying assumptions are that close interpersonal relations

1

constitute distinctive and important social phenomena and that a systematic coherent conceptualization of them is necessary in order to develop, appreciate, and modify them. The focus is on the close heterosexual dyad—the intimate relationship between man and woman. I believe (but do not attempt to demonstrate) that my concepts are applicable to any relationship we would regard as a personal one. The choice of the heterosexual dyad as the subject of analysis is dictated partly by the fact that it is the basis of most of the current knowledge about personal relationships. Additionally, in its various manifestations in dating, marriage, cohabitation, and romantic liaisons, the heterosexual dyad is probably the single most important type of personal relationship in the life of the individual and in the history of society. It occasions the greatest satisfactions of life and also the greatest disappointments. As the core of the family group, the heterosexual dyad sometimes generates the old-fashioned, warm, and supportive setting portrayed by the Waltons on television but too often creates the type of modern American home that was recently described in the media as being surpassed in violence only by a battlefield or a riot. Most important, especially in the family context, close heterosexual relationships constitute the most significant settings in which social attitudes, values, and skills are acquired and exercised.

In presenting this conceptualization of the close personal relationship I do not mean to suggest that it is the only possible way to view these relationships for scientific purposes. However, what follows does take account of what I believe to be the central and unique phenomena to be observed in such relationships. This can best be illustrated by considering two brief scenarios of important events within close relationships.

Consider first Bill and Jane, a young university couple. They have been going together off and on for almost two years, and Bill is deciding whether or not to ask Jane to marry him. If he does it means making a commitment to her, breaking off with old girlfriends, and giving up some of his current freedoms. He thinks over their times together and the things Jane has done for his sake. He remembers how wonderful she can make things for him. As he recalls these occasions, he realizes that they have often enjoyed the same things. At the same time he recognizes that some of the things she has done for his sake were probably not things she would have chosen to do herself. He also remembers similar occasions on which he has made sacrifices for her. He thinks of what a good person she is and, in view of her apparent joy at seeing him happy, how much she seems to love him. He senses that she has already made some commitment to him and will be receptive to the idea of extending that commitment into an exclusive relationship. He also knows his own pleasure at seeing her happy. So he decides he wants to "take the leap" (make the final commitment) and propose marriage.

In this example, we see evidence of three essential elements of the personal relationship:

(1) *Interdependence in the consequences of specific behaviors, with both commonality and conflict of interest:* Bill thinks of his dependence on Jane, as evidenced by the importance to him of specific things she had done for him and with him. His decision is

whether or not to let himself become more dependent. She also seems to be dependent on him. Though they may share many interests, there are also times in their relationship when what one wants is not what the other one prefers.

(2) *Interaction that is responsive to one another's outcomes:* On certain occasions when they have different interests, she has been aware of his desires and has set aside her own preferences and acted out of consideration of his. In lay language, she has "gone out of her way for him" or even perhaps "put up with a lot from him." To use other everyday terms, she has shown sensitivity to and considerateness of his needs.

(3) *Attribution of interaction events to dispositions:* Bill's decision follows his attribution to Jane of certain *stable* and *general* causes—her dispositions. These include stable preferences and interests compatible with his but, more important, attitudes of love toward him. Her love will last (in common parlance) "through thick and thin" and will "govern all"—that is, control her actions in a variety of situations. Bill probably also attributes stable attitudes to himself: for example, he feels he will always love her. Both the attributions to her and those to himself imply that he can accept his dependence on her and even permit it to increase.

The negative side of a personal relationship, shown in a conflict episode, involves the same three elements. The following incident is rather trivial and certainly less significant for the relationship than the preceding example, but it will serve our purpose. It concerns a small part of the lives of Mary and Dan, a young working couple who live together. Specifically, when Dan uses the bathroom he leaves it in a mess, with towels scattered around, a ring in the washbowl and tub, and so forth. Mary asks Dan not to mess up the bathroon in this manner. Two days later he repeats his usual performance as if Mary had said nothing. She becomes very angry. (On his side, he can't understand what she's so upset about. He had merely forgotten to do what she had asked.)

Referring to the three properties listed earlier:

(1) In this example we see Mary's side of the *interdependence*. Dan does something Mary strongly dislikes. Her outcomes are affected by his actions. There is also conflict of interest: Apparently he himself doesn't care about bathrooms being in a state of messiness or at least not enough to expend the effort to clean up after himself.

(2) There is a failure on Dan's part to be *responsive to her outcomes*. Knowing what she wants of him (in fact, having been told), he has failed to override his habits, preferences, or laziness out of consideration for her desires.

(3) The story doesn't say so explicitly, but Mary probably makes *attributions* of Dan's behavior to *stable dispositions*. Her version of the story is probably: "He repeats his usual performance as if I had said nothing." (Dan's version is that he merely forgot.) When subjects are asked to give explanations for the event as *she* describes it, not surprisingly a majority of them attribute it to Dan's stable properties: his traits (lazy, messy) or his attitude toward Mary (doesn't care about her wishes, doesn't like being told what to

do). If she entertains any of these beliefs about the person with whom she is living, Mary's anger is understandable.

In short, in this example of conflict we see the same three elements as in the earlier positive example. Here of course the conflict aspects of the interdependence figure prominently in the scenario. They provide the context within which Dan's lack of sensitivity and considerateness is apparent. This instance of failure on his part is interpreted by Mary in relation to past or recent events: his messy behavior and her request that he discontinue it. The attribution she finds appropriate for the event suggests that Dan's stable dispositions are not those of a person with whom an interdependent existence will be easy.

If we examine the three phenomena listed earlier and consider the relations among them, we gain two important insights into the relationship: First, *the participants make a partitioning of the causes for the events in their interaction.* That is, they make a distinction between the anticipated immediate incentives for behavior—its perceived direct consequences—and stable, general causes—what I have referred to as personal dispositions, which include attitudes, traits, and values. Second, *the participants assume that the dispositional causes are manifest in behavior that is responsive to the partner's outcomes and that therefore sometimes departs from the actor's own immediate interests.* These two aspects of the participants' beliefs about the causes of behavior in their relationship are shown schematically in Fig. 1.1 The partitioning of causes is shown at the left, the behavioral events in the interaction being affected jointly by

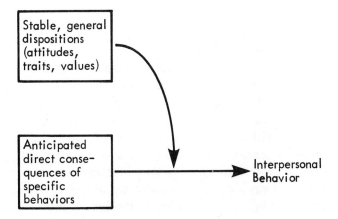

FIG. 1.1.   The participants' assumptions about the causes
of interpersonal behavior.

anticipated direct consequences and by dispositions.
The latter are seen to affect or modulate the causal
link between the direct consequences and the enacted
behavior. For this reason the dispositions are to be
inferred from discontinuities between the direct consequences to the actor and the behaviors he enacts.
These assumptions about the causes of interpersonal
behavior are most clearly apparent when the participants (a) scan behavior for how it departs from the
actor's own immediate interests (its direct consequences for him), (b) interpret such departures in
terms of the actor's responsiveness to the partner's
interests, and (c) explain patterns of this responsiveness in terms of such things as the actor's attitudes
toward the partner.

We now come to an important choice point in our
analysis. Are we to take the participants' assumptions
in Fig. 1.1 as reflecting merely a subjective reality or

"story" that they typically develop about their relationships but that has little to do with the hard realities of their interaction? Or are we to take them as reflecting the real, underlying structure of these relationships and therefore indicative of how *we* should conceptualize it? The former might be suggested by the comments of Weiss, Hops, and Patterson (1973) about conflictful marital relationships, that in most cases "a considerable amount of mutual training in vagueness has . . . taken place and . . . assumptions and expectations about the spouse overshadow the data at hand [p. 309]." The partners usually fail to label contingencies governing the mutual behavior, and "rely heavily upon a cognitive—motivational model of behavior. Thus, 'intent,' 'motivation for good or bad,' 'attitude,' etc., are all invoked to 'explain' the behavior of the other [p. 310]." Accordingly, the couple must be helped to set aside these explanations and to pinpoint the specific behavior-consequence-behavior sequences that get them into trouble.

Although admitting that the above view may be appropriate for relationships observed in clinical practice, I am inclined to take a different view of more typical personal relationships. Specifically, I emphasize that the subjective realities—the perceived intentions and attitudes—are of crucial significance in their development and functioning. Inappropriate causal explanations may indeed play a detrimental role in distressed relationships, and attention to specific behaviors and their consequences may be necessary if a battling couple is to break out of a vicious cycle of mutual aggression. However, in more normal relationships and particularly in those that attain high levels of mutual satisfaction, the "cognitive—motivational model of behavior" (as in Fig. 1.1) provides the basis for both their smooth functioning and the enjoyment of their deepest gratifications.

In short I have chosen to take Fig. 1.1 as indicating how the personal relationship should be conceptualized. The participants' scanning of behavior for its responsiveness to the partner's versus the actor's interests, and their explanation of this responsiveness in terms of stable dispositions constitute important processes that control behavior and affect in the relationship, are based on objective structures of the relationship, and give rise to other structures.

From this perspective we can review the concepts and evidence regarding the personal relationship under three headings (corresponding to the next three chapters) that parallel the three earlier points:

(1) *The structure of outcome interdependence:* This is an analysis of the interdependence between the persons in regard to their immediate concrete outcomes. This is the basic structural foundation of their relationship, defined by how they separately and jointly affect one another's direct outcomes.

(2) *The transformation of motivation: responsiveness to patterns of interdependence.* This is an analysis of the manner in which the persons' interaction is responsive to patterned aspects of their interdependence, each one's behavior being governed not only by his/her own outcomes but by the other's outcomes as well. By virtue of its partial independence of the actor's own immediate outcomes, pattern-responsive behavior constitutes in effect a transformation of the

interdependence structure defined by those outcomes. Thus we must consider the processes that give rise to and mediate such transformations.

(3) *The attribution and manifestation of interpersonal dispositions:* This analyzes the manifestation in interaction, and particularly in its departures from and transformations of the basic interdependence structure, of relatively stable and general properties of the two persons. These are referred to as interpersonal dispositions because of their unique relevance to interpersonal relations.

In reviewing the evidence under these three headings I present some of the facts that have led to the points emphasized in the foregoing. After examining these three sets of ideas we can finally return (in chapter 5) to our original problem and attempt to outline a model of the relationship. This constitutes a technical elaboration of Fig. 1.1 and a suggestion of the interrelations among the structures and processes it implies. At that point we consider how persons are interdependent in regard to their dispositional properties. Thus in our elaboration of Fig. 1.1 we consider interdependence not only at the specific level but at the general level as well and examine the relations between the two levels. Our model, then, is cast in terms of *levels of interdependence* and the processes linking the levels.

The concepts I employ are found for the most part in prior writings by John Thibaut and myself. These will be indicated where appropriate. To provide a historical context for the analysis, it may be noted that its three key ideas also occur in the writings of earlier social psychologists. The grandfathers for these focal concepts are, respectively, Lewin, Asch, and Heider. In his papers creating the field of group dynamics, Kurt Lewin (1948) emphasized that *interdependence* among its members is the essential, defining property of a group. Lewin specified interdependence in a variety of ways, but particularly appropriate for us is his description of interdependence in satisfying needs, exemplified in his analysis of marriage partners (pp. 84–102). From this notion stemmed Deutsch's conceptualization of interdependence between persons in locomotion toward their respective goals. We see later some of the consequences of the important comparison that Deutsch (1949) made between promotive *versus* contrient interdependence (roughly, a comparison of cooperative and competitive relationships).

The notion of *responsiveness to others' outcomes* is implicit in Solomon Asch's assertion (1959) that "an essential feature of social life [is] the capacity of individuals under some circumstances to transcend their own particular interests and to act in the interest of their group [p. 370]." He remarks that "It is of considerable consequence for any social psychology to establish the grounds of concern for the welfare of other persons or groups, and how these are related to the concern individuals feel for their own welfare [p. 368]." The concepts and analysis presented in chapter 3, abbreviated from Kelley and Thibaut (1978), constitute one attempt to deal with this problem. In his own consideration of the matter, Asch focuses on the concept of "mutually relevant fields," by which he means that each individual represents "to himself the situation that includes himself and others. These individual representations contain, in cases of full-fledged interaction, a reference to the fact that the others also possess a corresponding view of the situation [p. 371].'' In the present context, the latter is an essential fact underlying the individual's perception that others take account or fail to take account of his outcomes.

Attribution to dispositions is an idea directly adopted from Fritz Heider (1958). He emphasizes the principle that "man grasps reality, and can predict and control it, by referring transient and variable behavior and events to relatively unchanging underlying conditions, the so-called dispositional properties of his world [p. 79]." Heider notes that in the perception of persons, "the manifold of incoming messages (the proximal stimuli of perception) is encoded in terms of the motives, sentiments, beliefs, and personality traits of other persons. . . . these are dispositional properties, the relatively stable distal features that are relevant to us [p. 53]."

Our initial examples of the close personal relationship suggest that all three of these concepts are necessary in its characterization. The following chapters weave these concepts together as we attempt to construct a model of the personal relationship.

The Structure of Outcome Interdependence

2

Interdependence refers to the *effects* interacting persons have on each other. Interdependence can be described in many different ways depending on the nature of the effect in question. Thus we might define interdependence as mutual attitudinal influence, spread of emotional states (contagion), interchange of information, or, as suggested by Robert Sears (1951), mutual behavioral effects, each person's behavior providing the stimulus for the other's response.

In our book *The Social Psychology of Groups* (1959) Thibaut and I chose to define interdependence in terms of the affective consequences of interaction—its outcomes. The interdependence between persons is specified by how they control one another's outcomes, which include on the one hand rewards and benefits and on the other hand costs and punishments.

The analysis of interdependence in terms of outcomes has a general similarity to economic models of choice and to game-theoretic models of interaction. Consequently the analysis tends to draw the criticisms commonly directed to such models by social scientists—namely, that the theory (1) disregards the noneconomic consequences of interaction, taking no cognizance of altruism and similar humane social impulses, and (2) assumes unrealistically that people are rational and outcome-maximizing in their social behavior. We attempted to show that a social–psychological analysis of outcome interdependence need not be vulnerable to these criticisms. Concerning the alleged disregard of the noneconomic consequences of behavior, we argued that whatever the consequences of interaction and whatever the needs involved, whether egoistic or altruistic, they can be entered into the description of the interactors' outcomes. We further argued that although an outcome characterization of the interdependence may have implications for how persons *should* behave if they are to satisfy certain criteria such as that of maximum outcomes, the social psychologist need not assume, and would not be inclined to assume, that interaction is always characterized by such behavior. Because the conditions of interaction are often incompatible with reflection and deliberate choice, the actual course of interaction often reflects automatic behavioral sequences and internalized social routines. Although occasionally it may be characterized by simple choice guided by short-run outcome maximization, it also involves processes akin to cognitive problem-solving—recognizing outcome patterns and having insight into the modes of behavior necessary to achieve long-run solutions to the problems posed by interdependence. And of course interaction often falls short of yielding maximum outcomes because of imperfections in the interactors' understanding of the consequences of their behavior.

Whatever our final evaluation of the criticisms of defining interdependence in terms of outcomes, we must also recognize the important *benefits* derived from doing so. *First*, the description of a relationship in terms of how the persons affect each other's outcomes provides the framework within which a variety of interactions can be understood and, under certain conditions, predicted. This variety includes the implicit exercise of influence via classical and instrumental conditioning; the explicit exercise of influence via threats and promises; the processes of negotiation, bargaining, and compromise; and the development of coalitions within larger groups. It is difficult to see how this array of interaction processes could be conceptualized if we began, for example, with the definition of interdependence that Sears suggested, as stimulus–response sequences. *Second*, analysis of interdependence in terms of outcomes permits account to be taken of the affective consequences of interaction—for example, the feeling states (envy, pride) associated with conditions of relative deprivation or privilege or the frustration and anger deriving from nonvoluntary membership in unsatisfactory relationships. *Third*, and centrally important for the present analysis, a specification of interdependence in terms of outcomes defines the stimulus materials employed in the attributional and self-presentational process of interpersonal relations. As in my earlier examples, attributions of personal dispositions are importantly based on behavior in relation to the outcomes, both the actor's and the partner's, in the relationship. Similarly, certain key personal properties such as love or loyalty are displayed, both to the partner and to the external observers, by behavior that departs from certain of one's own outcomes and is responsive to certain outcomes of the partner.

EXAMPLES OF INTERDEPENDENCE

There is abundant evidence in scientific research on close relationships about the ways that the participants affect each other's outcomes. In our 1959 book Thibaut and I examined the sociometric literature for what it suggests to be the kind of rewards and costs that affect sociometric choices—that is, choices to associate with others as friends, in sharing living quarters, or as workmates. This was summarized as follows:

> Persons are chosen . . . if they are able and willing to help others in various ways and if others are able to act with a minimum of tension and restraint in their presence. On the other hand, persons are rejected if they fail to provide help to others (particularly if they are able but refuse to do so) or if they raise others' costs by inducing anxiety or discomfort. Abilities enter into this picture insofar as they enable one person, at low cost, to help another [p. 49].

The interpersonal attraction literature contains similar information. The things that attract us to others constitute a part of what makes us dependent on them. The bases of attraction suggest, then, the kinds of rewards or reduction in costs others can provide us. In the recent revision of their book *Interpersonal Attraction* (1978), Berscheid and Walster summarize the main bases of attraction. These have been shown to include:

(1) Liking us personally. (Others who hold us in high esteem provide a strong source of reward by expressing their evaluation.)

(2) Sharing our attitudes on social, economic, and political matters. (Such persons provide reward by offering a validation of our own views. They are also likely to hold us in esteem.)

(3) Providing emotional support when we are "lonely, fearful, or under stress." (Such persons reduce the costs of life by alleviating our anxiety and depression.)

The foregoing summaries suggest some of the actions of other persons, such as help or admiration, that have noncontingent effects on our rewards and costs, these effects being essentially independent of our own behavior. Thibaut and Kelley (1959, chapter 4) also describe the ways in which the effect of another person's action can be contingent on our own behavior. Behavioral interference and facilitation result in an individual's outcomes being determined jointly by his or her own and the partner's behavior. Later is presented further evidence of this joint determination of outcomes as well as its theoretical implications.

Another source of evidence on outcome interdependence, bearing on its more negative aspects, is provided by studies of interpersonal conflict. These examine the ways closely related people either raise each other's costs or withhold rewarding behavior from each other. Let us consider some evidence obtained from several studies of interpersonal problems and conflict.

The first of these is an interview study that John Cunningham, Harriet Braiker Stambul, and I conducted at U.C.L.A. in 1973. We interviewed 100 young heterosexual couples from the university community about the problems they had encountered in their relationships. The nearly 400 problems reported were grouped into 65 homogeneous categories. We were impressed with the diversity of problems and with the difficulty we had in trying to organize them into larger homogeneous clusters. We finally came up with the 15 categories listed in Table 2.1. The left column of percentages shows the distribution of the 400 problems over the 15 categories.

Also shown in Table 2.1 are data from a 1977 questionnaire study at U.C.L.A., conducted by Ronald Tiggle, Mark Peters, and myself. Members of young married couples were asked to give instances of the most important things they would like their partners to start doing or to discontinue doing. The 52 couples provided almost 700 such items. These were coded into the same specific categories as used for the earlier data and then grouped into the 15 broad types shown in Table 2.1.

No special merit is claimed for the particular way of categorizing the problems shown in Table 2.1. At this level of gross classification, there is considerable arbitrariness about the grouping, and intercoder agreement is not entirely satisfactory. (Independent coders agree about 60% of the time in their use of the 65 specific categories. When these categories are grouped

TABLE 2.1
Classification of Problems Reported by Heterosexual Couples

| Category | Percentages | |
	1973 Interview (100 couples)	1977 Questionnaire (52 couples)
1. Inadequate & poor communication	7.6	7.3
2. Aggressive behavior & temper	4.3	3.8
3. Influence attempts, nagging, making decisions	7.4	3.6
4. Failure to give appreciation, understanding, affection	12.5	11.9
5. Independence, external involvements	6.9	0.1
6. Dependence, possessiveness	3.1	3.3
7. Passivity, lack of confidence, lack of ambition	2.2	16.6
8. Excessive worry, compulsivity, moodiness	4.1	8.6
9. Carelessness, sloppiness, impulsivity	11.7	17.3
10. Conflicting preferences about leisure time, where & how to live, etc.	9.9	8.3
11. Division & fulfillment of responsibility	13.0	6.4
12. Interference with partner's study, work, etc.	4.6	2.3
13. Inappropriate behavior in social situations	4.3	4.4
14. Attitudes & behavior toward parents	5.6	1.7
15. Attitudes & behavior toward friends	2.6	3.5

into the 15 larger ones, the rate of agreement goes up to slightly over 70%.) However, the categories in Table 2.1 are not unlike those revealed by other studies (e.g., DeBurger, 1967; Goode, 1956; Levinger, 1966). They include what are obviously errors of commission constituted by behaviors that raise the partner's costs—for example, aggressive behavior, nagging, moodiness, sloppiness, and inappropriate social behavior. Also included are errors of omission consisting of withholding rewards—for example, failure to give appreciation or affection, failure to fulfill responsibilities.

Certain types of problems occur at different rates in the two studies. Although it is foolhardy to make comparisons between two samples separated by a four-year time period and assessed in different ways, these differences suggest an important point for us. An examination of the categories that differ between the two studies reveals that *specific* behaviors are more frequent in the first study and *personal dispositions* are more frequent in the second one. The latter include prominently passivity, lack of self-confidence, and lack of ambition (Category 7); compulsivity and susceptibility to bad moods (Category 8); and carelessness and impulsivity (Category 9). The differences between the two studies are probably to be traced to differences in the data-gathering method. In both studies we were trying to obtain specific instances of behavior, and considerable emphasis was given to this in the instructions. In the 1973 interview we were able to reemphasize this instruction and more or less enforce it. With the 1977 questionnaire procedure, this was not possible. The differing results suggest that, left to themselves, members of couples often cast their complaints in terms of personal dispositions.

We had already been impressed with this phenomenon in the 1973 interview study. Cunningham, Stambul, and I did our best to elicit statements of problems exclusively at the level of specific behaviors. Despite our efforts, over 40% of the problems were given in nonspecific terms, many of these referring to personal traits and attitudes. I have since discovered that we were simply encountering a phenomenon that is well known to behavior modification therapists working with marital conflict. The behavior modification approach requires a specific behavioral definition of the problem, referred to as "pin-pointing." However, therapists using this approach are repeatedly frustrated in their efforts to elicit such definitions from the marriage partners. In chapter 4 we return to the theoretical significance of this phenomenon.

We examined the categories in Table 2.1 for whether or not they differentiated the two sexes and for whether or not they occurred with different frequency in married couples as contrasted with living-together, or cohabiting, ones. (The 1973 sample included 50 couples of each type.) With a few exceptions each kind of problem was reported as often by the female member as by the male and as often by marriage partners as by cohabiting couples. By and large, as revealed in their spontaneous complaints, the sources of unhappiness seem rather similar for the two sexes and in the married and living-together relationships. In general the problems reflect the fact that two closely interdependent persons, without regard to their sex, have different preferences about the events that occur in their interaction. Conflict in these relationships is not primarily a "Battle of the Sexes." More important seem to be differences between the two persons that are unrelated, on the average, to their respective genders.

As it has been shown, the categories of problems listed in Table 2.1 indicate the many different types of rewards and costs that are involved in close relationships. More important (though not as obvious), the categories also indicate a basic fact about the structure of interdependence in these relationships. A close examination of the categories reveals that some of the conflicts between the two persons are in their preferences about the *individual behaviors* a given person should enact in their relationship. For example, in Categories 2 and 3 one person wants the other to be less aggressive or nagging. In Category 11 one wants the other to do more chores around the house. In contrast, certain other categories reflect the two persons' different preferences about their *joint activities*. This type of conflict is best illustrated by Category 12, which refers to problems of coordinating activities so that one person's activities do not interfere with, for example, the other's studying or sleeping, and by Category 10, which includes conflicts about when to have sex, choice of joint leisure time activities, and so on. A rough count of the items summarized in Table 2.1 reveals that problems related to *joint* activities account for about one-third of the problems in the 1973 study and one-sixth of those in the 1977 study. Thus the content of conflict suggests that the ongoing relationship involves not only the *individual* production of rewards and costs but also the *joint* generation of rewards and costs, the latter being consequences that neither person can create independently. One is reminded here of the distinction made earlier between outcomes that are produced solely by one person's behavior on the one hand and those that are contingent upon both persons' actions on the other. Behavioral interference and facilitation effects make it desirable for the two persons' actions to be coordinated, but conflict arises when the effects are different for the two persons so that different joint activities are preferred.

The fact that outcomes are controlled both by each person individually and by the pair jointly reveals a basic property of the structure of the outcome interdependence that characterizes close relationships. As I intend to demonstrate, it means that the pair faces not only problems of "exchange," that is, of each doing something for the other, but equally important, they face problems of "coordination," that is, of managing not to interfere with each other and to join together in mutually facilitative activities. To develop this point and its context, it is necessary to turn to some theoretical ideas.

PATTERNS OF INTERDEPENDENCE

The Social Psychology of Groups (1959) does not present a theory of rewards and costs, as is sometimes erroneously asserted. Its contribution was *not* to identify the reward and cost consequences of interaction.

Rather, it was to identify *patterns* of such consequences. Thibaut and I assumed that rewards and costs can be identified and roughly quantified. Proceeding from that assumption, we analyzed the variety of ways in which persons can be interdependent with respect to their rewards and costs. We conducted our analysis by means of the conceptual tool referred to as the ''payoff matrix'' or, as we describe it, the outcome matrix. This is simply a logical method for describing how each person's outcomes depend, in various ways, on his own actions and his partner's actions.

An example payoff matrix is provided in Fig. 2.1. This figure presents the portion of a young couple's life having to do with cleaning their apartment. The data summarized here were obtained in 1975 by Tim Patterson and myself from 100 young heterosexual couples from the UCLA undergraduate community, each couple having a relationship of 3 months or more in duration.

The man and woman independently answered a questionnaire that included among others a question that may be paraphrased as follows: ''Assume that you and your partner share an apartment. Cleaning it is a disagreeable job, but it has reached the point where it needs to be done. However, each of you has other time-consuming things to do [work, study, etc.]. Rate each of the following possible events as to the degree of satisfaction or dissatisfaction you would feel.'' The ratings were made on 21-point scales ranging from -10 for very dissatisfied to $+10$ for very satisfied. The four possible events, which correspond to the four cells in the figure, were: (1) Both

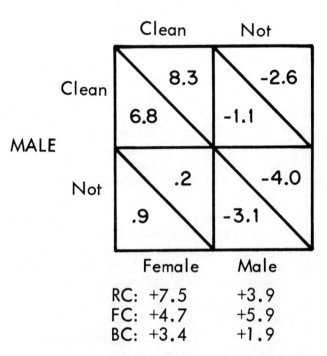

FIG. 2.1.   Rated outcomes for cleaning apartment (scale of −10 to +10).

of you clean; (2) You clean and your partner does other things; (3) You do other things and your partner cleans; and (4) You both do other things. The average ratings given by the 100 female respondents are shown in the upper portion of each cell, and the averages given by the 100 male partners are shown in the lower portion of each cell. The format conveniently shows how each person's outcomes are affected by the various actions and combinations of actions. Thus it is evident that the average female respondent is quite satisfied when both persons clean, close to neutral when she cleans and the partner does not, somewhat dissatisfied when she does not participate in the cleaning, and especially dissatisfied when the cleaning does not get done at all. The typical male respondent shows a correspondent pattern, with most satisfaction when both clean, nearly neutral feelings when his partner does it alone, and dissatisfaction if she does not participate at all. The existence of traditional sex-role attitudes in our average couple is shown by the fact that both persons are less happy when the man does the cleaning alone than when the woman does it alone.

Training in statistics teaches us that the variance in a table such as this can be analyzed into components. We can analyze the female's 2 × 2 table into three components: (1) A column effect that reflects how much difference on the average she can make in her own outcomes by varying her behavior; (2) a row effect reflecting how much on the average her outcomes are affected by her partner's actions; and (3) a column-by-row effect that reflects how much on the average her outcomes are affected by combinations of her own and the partner's actions. Similarly, we can analyze the male's 2 × 2 table into three components: a row effect, a column effect, and a row-by-column effect.

These analyses have been carried out in Fig. 2.2. The results presented there illustrate the three basic variance components of any outcome matrix. The first matrix shows how and the extent to which each person affects his/her own outcomes. The effect upon own outcomes is referred to as *reflexive control* inasmuch as it acts reflexively, back upon the person exercising it. The analysis shows that the woman gains 4.2 rating units when she cleans and loses 3.3 units when she does not. In other words, by her choice to clean or not, she exercises a reflexive control over her own outcomes of 7.5 units. Similarly, the man gains 2.8 units if he cleans and loses 1.1 units when he does not. His reflexive control, or effect on his own outcomes, is 3.9 units.

The second matrix shows the manner in which each person's outcomes are affected by the partner. The woman gains 2.8 units when the man cleans and loses 1.9 when he does not. Following Thibaut and Kelley (1959), this is referred to as *fate control*. Her fate is controlled by the man's choice to the extent of 4.7 units. She is subject to 4.7 units of fate control. Similarly, the man is subject to 5.9 units of fate control. He gains 3.8 units when she cleans and loses 2.1 units when she does not.

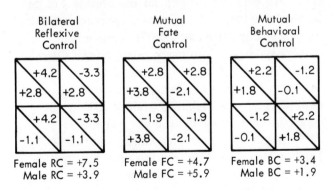

FIG. 2.2.   Variance components for cleaning the apartment.

The third matrix shows how each person's outcomes are determined by the *combinations* of their
actions. (These are the interaction terms in the two
analyses of variance.) Both gain units when the two
do the same thing (either *both* clean or *neither* cleans)
and lose units when one cleans and the other does not.
This pattern is referred to as *behavior control*. The
pattern of outcomes is such that if, for example, the
man were to change his behavior, the woman would
be motivated to make a corresponding change in hers.
In this particular case she gains units by matching her
behavior to his and loses units by failing to match his.

Any interdependence matrix can be analyzed into
the three components shown in Fig. 2.2. The first
shows how each person is affected reflexively by
his/her own actions, so it is called the *bilateral
reflexive control* (BRC) matrix. The second shows
how each person is affected in an absolute, noncontingent way by the partner's actions, so it is called the
mutual fate control (MFC) matrix. The third shows
how each person is affected by combinations of their
actions (by their joint actions), so it is called the
mutual behavior control (MBC) matrix.

We may now return to the original matrix and list
under it the components that account for the variance
of outcomes within it. The reflexive control (RC), fate
control (FC), and behavior control (BC) acting on
each person are given in the lower part of the Fig. 2.1.
As a matter of convention, each term is given a
positive sign if it refers to positive values in the upper
left cell and a negative sign otherwise. From Fig. 2.2,
it can be seen that all six terms in the example are
positive. This convention is necessary in order to take

account of the spatial orientation of the components relative to each other, as illustrated in the following. The terms for the various components reveal that the man is subject to more *fate control* than the woman is (he cares more what she does than she cares what he does) and that she is subject to more *reflexive control* than he is (she cares more what she herself does than he cares what he himself does). Both are more affected by her choice than by his. This is another way of expressing their mutual tendency to adopt a traditional sex norm in regard to household chores.

To repeat, any interdependence matrix can be analyzed into these three variance components. Examples of each of the three are shown schematically in Fig. 2.3. This shows BRC matrices in which each person's outcomes are affected by own actions, MFC matrices in which each one's outcomes are affected by the partner's actions, and MBC matrices in which each one's outcomes are affected by their joint actions. The last is shown in two forms: *correspondent* ones, in which the two persons have the same preferences for joint actions—their BC terms have the same signs—and a *noncorrespondent* one, in which they have different preferences—their BC terms have different signs. A simple example of the latter, in which one person prefers to match actions and the other prefers not to match them, is provided by the children's game of hide-and-seek.

In the BRC matrix of course the two persons are not interdependent. Each simply affects his/her own outcomes. However, the BRC component is very important to the relationship in how it is oriented to the other two components. These patterns vary not only

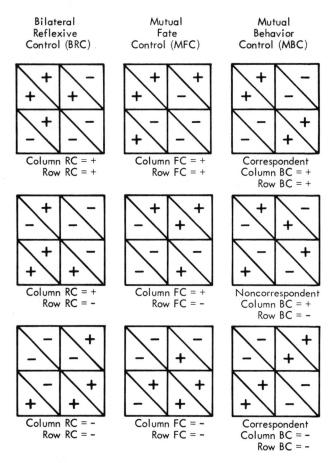

FIG. 2.3. Examples of the basic components of interdependence.

in their magnitude but in their orientation to one another, which is indicated by the signs of their terms. Thus the BRC pattern can be combined in a concordant way with the other patterns or in a discordant way. For example, Fig. 2.4 shows it combined concordantly and discordantly with MFC, the result being either a perfectly cooperative pattern, in which the two persons' outcomes are perfectly correspondent (positively correlated), or a perfectly competitive (constant-sum) pattern, in which their outcomes are perfectly noncorrespondent (negatively correlated). The well-known Prisoner's Dilemma game (PDG) is composed of discordant BRC and MFC components as in the lower portion of Fig. 2.4, but the magnitude of the FC terms is greater than that of the RC terms.

Interdependence derives wholly from the MFC and MBC components of the outcome matrices. Thus *MFC and MBC constitute the two basic aspects of interdependence*—that is, the interdependence properties of all outcome patterns are reducible to MFC, MBC, or combinations of them. This fact will enable the reader to understand why so much emphasis was given earlier to conflicts about both *individual* behavior and *joint* activities. We saw that the content of conflict involves both (1) problems of each *individual* doing what is rewarding to the other, or MFC, and (2) problems of coordinating on mutually rewarding *joint* activities, or MBC. In MFC the two persons have an opportunity to do something *for* one another, and their problem is whether or not they can work out an *exchange* of these benefits. In MBC they have an opportunity to do something *with* one another, and their problem is whether or not they can work out a *coordination* of their respective actions.

As an aside, it might be noted that having made this important distinction, Thibaut and I are reluctant to describe interdependence exclusively in terms of "exchange" and are uncomfortable about having our theory described as an "exchange" theory. It is equally a "coordination" theory. More accurately, it

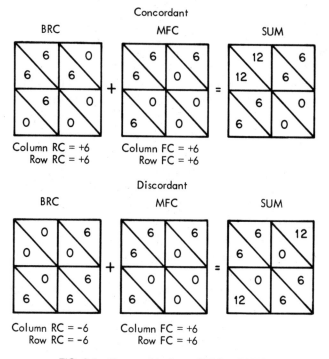

FIG. 2.4.   Two combinations of BRC and MFC.

is a general analysis of social interdependence, that is, a theory of interdependence.

Not only can any outcome matrix be analyzed into these three types of components but all possible matrices can be constructed by combining these three components in the various ways possible and in varying magnitudes. In our recent book (*Interpersonal Relations: A Theory of Interdependence*, 1978) Thibaut and I use the components analysis to explore all the possible patternings of interdependence that can be described by the 2 × 2 outcome matrix. These patterns are identified and then classified with respect to their properties, again with the aid of the component analysis. The result is a delineation of the domain of 2 × 2 matrices, the dimensions or properties of that domain, and the location within it of the 20 or so most important types of patterns (e.g., PDG, Turn-Taking Game, Zero-Sum games, Battle of the Sexes, Chicken, Threat Game, etc.).

The theoretical analysis shows that the four major properties of interdependence patterns are as follows:

(1) *Mutuality of dependence:* whether there is *mutual* dependence (*inter*dependence) or *unilateral* dependence;

(2) *Degree of dependence:* the degree to which the one or two persons are dependent on their partners;

(3) *Correspondence of outcomes:* the degree to which the outcomes of the two persons are correspondent or noncorrespondent; and

(4) *Basis of dependence:* whether the dependence in the relationship involves FC, BC, or some combination of the two.

Our general hypothesis is that the properties of the various 2 × 2 matrices reflect the important variations in the ways two persons can be interdependent—in the structure of their interdependence. If this hypothesis is valid, we should find *first* that the properties of these matrices listed in the foregoing correspond to the properties that differentiate real dyadic relationships. *Second*, the four properties should be related in a systematic manner to various aspects of the interaction processes observed in different kinds of real dyads. I wish now to consider some of the evidence bearing on these two points.

DIMENSIONS AND DISTRIBUTION
OF DYADIC RELATIONSHIPS

If the matrix analysis is relevant to interpersonal relationships, the properties with respect to which outcome matrices are differentiated should correspond to the properties with respect to which interpersonal relationships are differentiated. That is, interpersonal relationships should vary with respect to mutuality of dependence, degree of dependence, correspondence of outcomes, and the basis of interdependence.

The most useful data on this point come from a study by Wish, Deutsch, and Kaplan (1976). It not only provides evidence about the differentiating properties of real relationships but it permits us to test some hypothesis about the distribution of dyads in relation to those properties. The limitation of the data is that they reflect the *perceived* dimensions of interpersonal relationships. Subjects were asked to rate a number of relationships (e.g., close friends, siblings, business rivals, and teammates) on a number of semantic differential scales (e.g., very friendly vs. very hostile, always harmonious vs. always clashing). The results were analyzed by the method of multidimensional scaling, INDSCAL (Carroll & Chang, 1970), to reveal the distinctions the subjects make among the various relationships. The analysis yielded four dimensions. If the properties of interdependence patterns make for important variations in the interaction process, we would expect the properties to be reflected in the terms with which people differentiate kinds of relationships. This assumes of course that an entire relationship can be characterized by a single matrix or at least by a delimited set of matrices. Any extensive relationship, such as between two siblings, encompasses many areas and kinds of interdependence. Yet it is possible that a relationship of this sort takes its meaning from the one or two interdependence patterns that are most characteristic of its various problems and situations.

Consistent with this reasoning, the perceived dimensions of interpersonal relations derived by Wish, Deutsch, and Kaplan correspond for the most part to the matrix properties. The first dimension, "equal vs. unequal," was best defined by ratings on "exactly equal vs. extremely unequal power." At the *equal* end were the relationships of close friends, business partners, and so forth, and at the *unequal* end master and servant, parent and child, and the like. Inasmuch as differences in dependence give rise to differences in power (see next section), the dimension of "equal vs. unequal" corresponds to mutuality of dependence: mutual dependence vs. unilateral dependence. The second dimension, "intense vs. superficial," was best defined by "very active vs. very inactive" and "intense vs. superficial interaction with each other." At the *intense* end were husband—wife and parent—child relationships, and at the *superficial* end were casual acquaintances, second cousins, and the like. This dimension seems to reflect the degree of interdependence (or dependence) in the relationship, the intense relationship being one of high interdependence or dependence. The third dimension, "cooperative and friendly vs. competitive and hostile," was best defined by "always harmonious vs. always clashing," "compatible vs. incompatible goals and desires," and similar scales. At the *cooperative* end are close friends and husband and wife and at the *competitive* end political opponents, business rivals, and, interestingly, divorced couples. This dimension clearly reflects the correspondence versus noncorrespondence of outcomes in the relationship.

Wish, Deutsch, and Kaplan describe their fourth dimension as "socioemotional and informal vs. task-oriented and formal." It is primarily defined by a rating scale of "pleasure-oriented vs. work-oriented" and secondarily by "very informal vs. very formal" and "emotional vs. intellectual." At the *socioemotional* extreme are close friends, siblings, and marriage partners, and at the *task-oriented* extreme are such relationships as interviewer—job applicant, business rivals, and supervisor—employee. This dimension probably reflects in part a property of interdependent relationships to be explained later: the degree to which personal attitudes and dispositions are involved—that is, the degree to which the relationship is a personal one. Our model of the *personal* relationship, described in chapter 5, assumes that the attitudes and dispositions the persons display in their interactions constitute an important source of mutual reward and control over the interaction. Such relationships are to be contrasted with more "economic" ones, in which attitudes count for little and what is important are the specific behaviors and their direct consequences (goods, services, etc.).

Only our distinction between FC- and BC-based relationships is not reflected in the dimensions identified by Wish, Deutsch, and Kaplan. One possible reason for its absence is that most complex relationships involve both bases of interdependence and hence contain both types of problems. We see evidence of this later in Ivan Steiner's commentary (1972) on problem-solving groups.

The logical analysis of interdependence patterns suggests not only the major dimensions of interpersonal relationships but also how they should be distributed in the space defined by those dimensions. One implication of the analysis is that over all possible *inter*dependent patterns (those characterized by mutual dependence), the theoretical relation between degree of interdependence and correspondence of outcomes is approximately as in Fig. 2.5. This configuration reflects the simple fact that if two persons are independent they can have neither correspondence nor noncorrespondence of outcomes. Only if they become interdependent is it possible for them to have on the one hand an extremely cooperative relationship or on the other hand an extremely competitive one. In general, the more interdependent they become, the greater the degree to which their outcomes may be correspondent or noncorrespondent.[1]

To test this theoretical implication with the data from Wish, Deutsch, and Kaplan, their superficial – intense and cooperative – competitive dimensions were

---

[1]This statement must be qualified somewhat. It is strictly true only for relationships based on MBC. For those based on MFC, maximum variability in correspondence occurs with medium interdependence. For relationships involving both MBC and MFC, which probably include most real-life dyads, the distribution in Fig. 2.5 is generally appropriate. Details are to be found in chapter 4 of Kelley and Thibaut (1978).

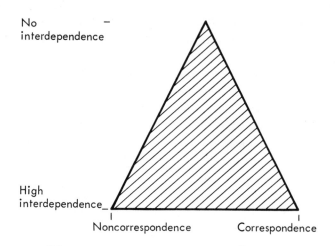

No — interdependence

High interdependence_

Noncorrespondence   Correspondence

FIG. 2.5.   Theoretical relation between degree of interdependence and correspondence vs. noncorrespondence of
outcomes.

assumed to correspond, respectively, to degree of
interdependence and correspondence — noncorrespondence. Fig. 2.6 shows the distribution of the equal
relationships on these two dimensions. It can be seen
that the observed distribution is largely consistent with
the expected one (Fig. 2.5). The relationships on the
intense side of the superficial — intense scale show
greater variance on the cooperative — competitive scale
than do those on the superficial side. However, the
relations on the cooperative side of the scale involve
somewhat higher degrees of intensity than those on
the competitive side. This is consistent with the
notion that people avoid relationships of high interdependence if they are also characterized by sharp
conflict of interest. More generally, whereas the
theoretical distribution in Fig. 2.5 is based on the

occurrence of all possible interdependence patterns, some of these patterns are not stable as they occur in natural pairings.

The Wish, Deutsch, and Kaplan data apply to different types of relationships and are consistent with the idea that their variability in correspondence – noncorrespondence of outcomes is greater the more closely interdependent the relationship. The results also show that marriage relationships and similar

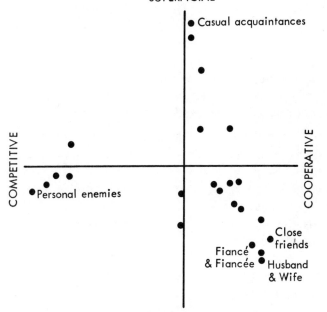

FIG. 2.6. Distribution of equal relationships on the dimensions of cooperativeness-competitiveness and superficial-intense. (Adapted from Wish, Deutsch, and Kaplan, 1976.)

personal relationships (between fiancé and fiancée, and close friends) are in the lower right region of Fig. 2.6. One then wonders about variations within this class of close relationships, and whether or not interdependence and commonality vs. conflict of interest are correlated across such pairings. Two possibilities are shown in Fig. 2.7. In Case I correspondence and interdependence are positively related, the scatterplot conforming to the general shape of the triangular distribution. This correlation also conforms to our common sense understanding that the closer a relationship is, the better the pair gets along and the fewer conflicts they have. In contrast, as in Case II, the two variables may not be correlated. This scatter plot would mean that as persons get closer, their relationship does not necessarily improve. In some cases people become increasingly divergent in their interests and in other cases increasingly convergent,

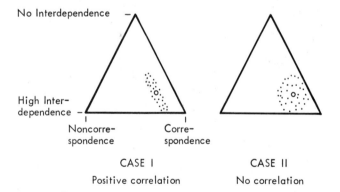

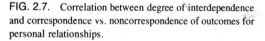

FIG. 2.7.   Correlation between degree of interdependence and correspondence vs. noncorrespondence of outcomes for personal relationships.

but on the average there is no relation between degree of interdependence and degree of conflict. In her thesis research on the development of close relationships leading to marriage, Harriet Braiker Stambul (1975) found evidence favoring Case II, a lack of relationship. Factor analysis of a series of questions about the relationship yielded two principal factors, Love and Conflict–Negativity, and these factors were not correlated. They were independent dimensions with respect to which the premarital and marital relationships could be distinguished. Stambul's Love scale included items indicating feelings of love, belonging, closeness, commitment, and attachment, as well as reports of need for the partner and of giving much to the relationship. On the face of it this is a plausible measure of degree of dependence on the partner. Stambul's Conflict–Negativity scale included items indicating frequency and seriousness of arguments, attempts to change the partner, and feeling and communicating anger to the partner. The lack of correlation between these two scales suggests that conflict does not decline with increasing interdependence (as in Case I) but bears no systematic relation to the degree of interdependence (Case II).

One may not be much impressed with the lack of correlation between two such scales because it may reflect small sample size and similar artifacts. However, there is other evidence, from an earlier study by Orden and Bradburn (1968), that is also inconsistent with Case I and consistent with Case II. Case I implies that a particular couple, at a given level of interdependence, will experience a narrow range of correspondent vs. noncorrespondent situations, some-what as indicated by the width of the scatter plot. From this it follows that within a sample of couples varying in degree of interdependence, the number of corre-spondent experiences should be negatively correlated with the number of noncorrespondent experiences. The more interdependent the couple, the more often they would experience correspondent outcomes and the less often noncorrespondent ones. In contrast, Case II implies that these two variables will be uncorrelated. In their study of dimensions of marital happiness, based on a large national sample, Orden and Bradburn found evidence consistent with Case II. The number of pleasurable activities a married couple was reported to have shared recently (which seems to be a reason-able index of frequency of experienced correspon-dence of outcomes) was not correlated with the number of things about which they had had problems during the same period (a clear index of frequency of noncorrespondent outcomes).

It must be noted that Stambul as well as Orden and Bradburn were studying members of intact marriages. In both studies the evidence suggests that increasing interdependence does not entail decreasing conflict. The triangular plot in Figs. 2.6 and 2.7 implies that the possibilities both for convergence of interest and for conflict of interest increase as interdependence increases. Apparently even members of successful marriage relationships are not able, with increasing interdependence, to restrict their interactions to the portions of their relationship characterized by com-monality of interest.

IMPLICATIONS OF INTERDEPENDENCE FOR INTERACTION PROCESS[2]

As noted earlier, our analysis of the domain of 2 × 2 matrices assumes that they reveal the most important variations in the ways two persons can be interdependent. The varieties of interdependence structure reflect both the different types of problems that persons encounter in their relationships and their means (via mutual influence) for dealing with those problems. Any particular pattern of interdependence has latent within it certain possible courses of interaction—plausible scenarios of action and reaction, communication (requests, complaints, threats, promises), and the associated feelings. These scenarios are not necessarily fully acted out by the participants. Their mutually recognized possibility and appropriateness to the situation govern the actual course of its events. With respect to explicit communication, for example, the structure of interdependence determines the things about which communication is necessary and sets limits on what communications are plausible. With shared understanding of the structure, much such communication is highly predictable and therefore unnecessary. The end state of an explicit interchange is fully anticipated, and the participants move directly to it without going through the intervening steps.

---

[2]The arguments in this section must be qualified later, when we develop our complete model of the personal relationship. The theoretical implications presented here apply to properties of what is defined in chapter 3 as the *effective* matrix.

We now consider the relevance of each of the four properties of interdependence for these interaction scenarios and for the consequences of interaction. This relevance can be documented in each instance by reference to some of the most pertinent empirical literature.

Unilateral Dependence

In relationships of unilateral dependence as compared with ones of mutual dependence there is latent a scenario of dissolution initiated by the less dependent person. This follows from the fact that the less dependent person is more likely to find something better to do with the time and effort required by the interaction. Evidence of this phenomenon is provided by Hill, Rubin, and Peplau (1976) from a study of over 200 dating couples who were followed over a 2-year period after initial assessment of their relationships. Couples who initially showed unequal involvement in their relationships (asymmetric dependence) were found more often to have broken up over the 2-year period. Furthermore, it was mainly the less involved person who precipitated the breakup. The potentiality of this scenario is also apparent in relationship measurements taken at one time. Thus in a questionnaire study of 150 romantically involved college couples Gregory White (1977) found that the less involved person sees a greater likelihood of dating and having sex with some one other than the current partner. Of course it is not always the less dependent person who is responsible for the breakup. There is another scenario in which the more involved one gets so little out of the relationship because of exploitation, rejection, or lack of reciprocation by the less dependent person that the former initiates the dissolution. The lesser dependence of the one person derives from that person's having activities and relationships that constitute attractive and plausible alternatives to the present one. White's data show that the less involved member of the couple has more opposite-sex friends and is more likely currently to have a relationship with one of those friends. The other side of this aspect of the scenario is obvious: The more dependent partner feels jealous and perceives the other partner's friends as threats to the present relationship. White finds the more dependent person to perceive greater threat from the partner's opposite-sex friends even when the partner is not thought presently to be involved with any of them.

The asymmetry in dependence sets the stage for the less dependent person to exercise more influence in the relationship. This aspect of the scenario has been stated by Waller and Hill (1951) as the Principle of Least Interest and conceptualized by Thibaut and Kelley (1959) in terms of the relation between a person's Comparison Level for Alternatives and Fate Control over the partner. Peplau (1977) reports evidence consistent with these ideas from the study of dating couples she conducted with Rubin and Hill (1976). The person judged to be less involved in the relationship tended also to be reported as the one having more "say." This was also reported to be true of the person with the lower score on the Liking and Loving Scale, the more attractive person, and the one with an alternative partner. In the present view these are merely different measures of the two persons' relative dependence on each other.

Results that seem to have the same theoretical significance come from studies of family power, a line of research begun by Blood and Wolfe (1960). Several studies have found husbands with greater socioeconomic resources (occupational prestige, educational achievement, income) to play a greater role in making decisions in the family. This finding has not been replicated in several other samples, the probable explanation being that the dynamics of the interdependence structure local to the relationship are overridden by strong cultural norms about family decision-making. (The effects of these norms upon the relationship can perhaps be understood by reference to concepts developed in chapter 4 of the present volume.) From their side, wives employed outside the home have been found to have more influence in financial decisions that women who are merely housewives. In one of the relevant studies, conducted on a sample of husbands and wives in Greece, those wives who reported that their husbands were more in love than they were themselves claimed to have more say in family matters than wives who felt themselves to be the ones more in love. Similar but nonsignificant trends were found for the husbands. By a variety of indications then, it appears that unless other factors intervene, the less dependent marriage partner tends to have the greater influence in the relationship. (For a brief review of the family power literature, see Aldous, 1977.)

In general the more dependent person may have to

settle for poor outcomes and tolerate high costs. In the extreme this may even entail putting up with violence at the hands of the partner, as Scanzoni (1978) suggests to be true for wives who have few alternatives to remaining in the marriage. At some point of course this affords the basis for the secondary dissolution scenario suggested above, in which it is the more dependent person who breaks up the relationship.

One might expect from the preceding comments to find the less dependent person to be the more openly domineering or directive in the interaction. However, as noted in the remarks introducing this section, when the structure of interdependence is understood in the same way by the two persons, its associated scenario need not occur in its full-blown form. In the present context this means that the less involved person need not exercise greater open and explicit influence. The more involved one will often anticipate the other's wishes and even be the one to initiate or propose what the partner desires. In the extreme case the more involved person sets aside his/her own desires and becomes highly responsive to the partner's outcomes. An apt illustration of this is provided by Peplau's description (1977) of the more involved Warren in his relationship with the less involved Jill: "Jill told us that 'Warren would do anything I want.' He gets himself to want to do the things she likes, and lets her make most decisions. . . . 'I wish he wouldn't spoil me. I come first, he's a distant second as far as he's concerned' [p. 17]." We see here evidence of "responsiveness" to the partner's outcomes, a topic to be considered more fully in the next chapter.

Degree of Interdependence

If we compare mutually dependent persons who are highly interdependent with those who are less so, the expected scenario for the latter includes the possibility of disruption. The longitudinal study reported by Hill, Rubin, and Peplau (1976) found that "in general those couples who were less intimate or less attached to one another when the study began were more likely to break up [p. 151]." Levinger's (1976) summary of the evidence on divorce similarly suggests that relationship dissolution is more probable when interdependence is low. There are many complexities in these data and many qualifications to be made, but divorce tends to occur when the rewards from the dyad are low, the costs of leaving the marriage are low, and rewards from outside alternatives are high.

With high interdependence the interaction scenario depends greatly on the correspondence versus noncorrespondence of outcomes (see next section). Given a considerable degree of correspondence, the only case to be considered here, we can expect the two persons to be motivated to accommodate their (small) differences and get along with one another. Each one is willing to yield to the other's desires and yet, when the mutual dependence is recognized, able to perceive the partner to be similarly willing. When differences arise, there exists for each person the intrapersonal conflict of "change or be changed" (Kelley & Thibaut, 1969). Accordingly we can expect a scenario of active exertion of influence and counterinfluence that ultimately results in reconciliation of differences and uniformity of views and behavior. An early study of this phenomenon by Kurt Back (1951) is still one of the most informative. Back experimentally created dyads with high and low cohesiveness, these being variations in the degree to which the two persons were dependent on one another for various rewards. Each dyad was given a task that required the pair to resolve certain differences between themselves. The highly cohesive pairs showed greater final convergence in their views but also, as suggested in the scenario referred to in the foregoing, greater overt resistance to each other's suggestions during the course of their interaction. The relation between cohesiveness (interdependence) and agreement within the pair is consistent with much evidence from larger groups, that cohesive ones are characterized by uniformity of attitudes and behavior. Cartwright and Zander (1968) provide a summary of this literature.

Correspondence of Outcomes

With high commonality of interest, in which what the partner wants tends to be the same as what you want, a common scenario will be one of much communication that is both trustworthy (honest) and trusted (taken at face value). For example, in the case of correspondent MBC (Fig. 2.3) each person will be eager to know what the other intends to do, willing honestly to state own behavioral intentions, and ready to believe the other's similar statements. The contrast is provided by noncorrespondent MBC. If the reader can visualize this pattern as a game of hide-and-seek (the column person being the hider and the row person the seeker, there being only two places where the former can hide and the latter can seek), the scenario associated with the pattern will be apparent. There is no reason for either person to communicate honestly to the other (e.g., telling where one intends to hide) or to believe anything the other may say.

Deutsch's (1949) comparison of promotive interdependence and contrient interdependence consists primarily in an examination of the communication differences associated with correspondent and noncorrespondent relationships. Five-man groups were assembled from a university class to hold discussions and solve problems. Correspondence of outcomes was created in some groups by making individual course grades contingent on the quality of the group's performance. In other groups noncorrespondence was created by the rule that grades would be determined entirely by comparisons of individual performance within each group. The results were in line with the trust and distrust scenarios described in the foregoing. The correspondent groups showed more effective intergroup communication, with greater attentiveness to and ease of understanding each other and greater mutual influence. They also exhibited greater coordination of effort, which would suggest the role of correspondent MBC in the interdependence of these groups.

Patterns of intermediate correspondence (neither correspondent nor noncorrespondent) differ from both of the extreme cases in that they provide the basis for a scenario of negotiation or bargaining. These intermediate cases have often been referred to as "mixed-motive games," because they evoke mixtures of cooperative and competitive motivation. An example is shown in Fig. 2.8 and should be compared with the patterns of correspondent and noncorrespondent MBC in Fig. 2.3. In the correspondent case there is nothing to bargain about: What one wants is wholly acceptable to the other one. In the noncorrespondent case there is no basis for bargaining: To the degree that one person wants something, the partner does not want it. Only in patterns such as Fig. 2.8, where there are some things they can agree about (e.g., to avoid the mutually negative cells in the matrix) and other things they disagree about (e.g., which of the two positive

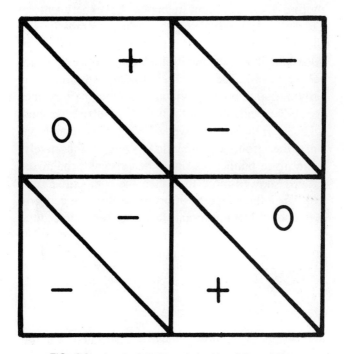

FIG. 2.8.   A mixed-motive relationship of intermediate degree of correspondence.

outcomes to obtain), is there a basis for bargaining. In the example in Fig. 2.8, an agreement can be struck on some trade-off between the two positive outcomes, provided that repeated interaction within the matrix is possible.

In short, with patterns intermediate between the correspondent and noncorrespondent extremes, negotiation becomes an expected component of the interaction scenario, this being a process that enables the persons to resolve the dilemmas associated with protecting their respective individual interests and promoting their common interest. An experiment by Zander and Wolfe (1964) provides a comparison of the intermediate or mixed case with the extremes of correspondence (cooperation) and noncorrespondence (competition). The mixed relationship was created by providing that both individual and group performance would be made known to important outside persons, whereas in the cooperative and competitive conditions only the group or individual scores, respectively, were made public. As might be expected, the mixed groups showed more trust than the competitive ones but less interchange of information than the cooperative ones. Most important, there was more procedural negotiation and transferring of performance points from one person to another (a sign of bargaining) in the mixed groups than in either of the other two types.

Basis of Interdependence

The basic interaction scenarios associated with FC and BC depend of course upon the correspondence or noncorrespondence of outcomes. Here I consider the case of correspondence. With correspondent MBC (Fig. 2.3) one person might be heard to say, "Let's do *this* together," and the other to reply, "Fine." Alternatively one person will take the initiative by acting in a definitive manner, and the partner, observing this, will coordinate appropriately. When there are obstacles to observing each other's actions, the pair will develop schedules and rules of action that make possible the necessary coordination even in the absence of communication or behavioral surveillance.

With MFC (Fig. 2.3), a standard scenario will involve one person's saying, "I'll do *this* for you if you'll do *that* for me" and the other's compliance. Often there are counterconsiderations acting on one or both persons that work against exercising FC to the benefit of their partners. These discordant RC factors are constituted by such diverse things as ineptitude, laziness, and the attractions of competing activities. Any or all of these may conspire to induce one person in an MFC-based exchange to become a "freeloader," receiving benefits from the partner without returning them. Here, as in other instances, the reader will have little difficulty in generating the resulting scenario, with its complaints, threats, promises, and so on. Some of the reactions of other group members to the freeloader are suggested by experiments summarized by Kelley and Thibaut (1969, pp. 32–33).

Most real-life relationships probably involve both FC and BC as the bases of their interdependence, these being separately operative in different domains of the interaction or in combination (as in Fig. 2.8) in other domains. This fact is implied by our study of conflict problems in which the young couples mentioned both types of problems. It is also strongly suggested by Ivan Steiner's (1972) analysis of group process in problem-solving groups. In analyzing the "process losses" that are incurred in such groups, Steiner distinguishes between (1) losses from lack of "interpersonal coordination, matching, and temporal programming" and (2) losses from inadequate member motivation to make high quality contributions to the group. The first clearly refers to coordination problems created by MBC. The second reflects the role of MFC in combination with discordant BRC, as in the PDG or the perfectly competitive, discordant MFC + BRC pattern (See Fig. 2.4). As in the freeloading scenario mentioned earlier, the person prefers not to enact the behaviors that are desired by other members, either for reasons of laziness or other cost-avoidance motives or because alternative behaviors are more rewarding. As Steiner describes it, "members are unwilling to make full use of their resources, and thus contribute poor individual outcomes to the group [p. 83]." Steiner analyzes the effects of group size and its relation to these two types of process loss. In the present context I am interested simply in noting that the two bases of interdependence provide a theoretical basis for the two types of loss he distinguishes.

This chapter has been a brief overview of the relevance to dyadic interaction process of the theoretically identified properties of interdependence structures. These structures also provide the settings in which various norms and values develop and are applied. Furthermore, the outcome patterns constitute the context in which various interpersonal attitudes and traits are expressed—the *ground* upon which such dispositions appear as *figures*. With the addition of values, attitudes, and traits to the dynamic factors operative in the dyad, some of the interaction scenarios outlined in the foregoing are greatly modified. Some of these complexities are considered in the following chapters.

The Transformation of Motivation: Responsiveness to Patterns of Interdependence

3

In the preceding chapter I reviewed concepts and evidence relating to the pattern of interdependence, which is a description of the basic structural properties of the personal relationship. It was shown that this pattern is causally related to many of the important interaction phenomena in the relationship, including such aspects as the mutual influence and the degree of conflict experienced. I now look more closely into the question of exactly how the interdependence structure is linked to behavior.

In his 1959 contribution to the volume in the Koch series that dealt with social psychology, Solomon Asch described what he saw as "a problem in motivation which belongs at the very center of the discipline [p. 368]." This problem involves identifying the bases of the concern that individuals show for the welfare of other persons and understanding how this concern relates to the concern individuals have about their own welfare. The present chapter deals with a proposed solution to this problem, specifically the one presented by John Thibaut and myself in our book *Interpersonal Relations: A Theory of Interdependence* (1978).

It is a basic fact of social life that people are responsive not only to their own outcomes but also to the outcomes of other people. As Asch wrote, "the need or goal of one person can, given certain conditions, arouse forces in another person toward fulfilling them, without exclusive reference to the latter's 'own' needs [p. 373]." This is made possible in Asch's view by the individual's capability for "representing to himself the situation that includes himself and others [p. 371]."

These comments imply that there exists a cognitive link between the interdependence matrix and behavior—a link that involves perceiving the pattern of outcomes (other's outcomes as well as one's own) and responding to certain aspects of that total pattern. This cognitive link was represented in several ways in Thibaut and Kelley's *The Social Psychology of Groups* (1959) but primarily in the concept of the Comparison Level (CL). This concept refers to the tendency of people to compare their obtained outcomes with the level of outcomes they believe they deserve from the relationship. This comparison is often made with the outcomes other persons are experiencing. In a close dyadic relationship the partner's outcomes may figure prominently in the individual's CL. Under these conditions there is comparison with the partner and a calibration of the individual's own outcomes in relation to those of the partner. If own outcomes surpass those of the partner, the person is satisfied, but if own outcomes fall short of the partner's, the person is dissatisfied. This constitutes of course a specific kind of "taking account" of the total pattern of outcomes. Making this comparison produces a modification of one's response. Minimally, one's affective response to own outcomes is changed, as for example when certain outcomes once thought to be good are later received with dissatisfaction upon learning that the other person's outcomes are better. There may also be an effect on one's behavior, as when one tries to do something to rectify the situation of below-CL outcomes.

EVIDENCE OF PATTERN RESPONSIVENESS

Laboratory demonstrations and assessments of pattern responsiveness have been plentiful in recent years. For example, Charles McClintock and his colleagues have shown that behavior in interdependent games is affected by knowledge of the other player's outcomes (McClintock & McNeel, 1966). The usual result is that such knowledge produces an increase in competitive behavior, which suggests a comparison effect of the type just described.

Robert Wyer (1969) asked subjects who were anticipating playing a laboratory game with an unknown partner to rate the desirability of various *pairs* of their own and the partner's score outcomes. Thus they indicated how desirable it would be if they received +2 points and the other received −3 points or if they received −4 points and the other +3 points, and so forth. By a least squares procedure Wyer calculated how a person's desirability ratings related to his own and the partner's points—that is, what weights were given to own score and to other's score. The best-fitting linear function showed that own score was weighted about

+0.75 and partner's score was weighted about −0.40. In other words the typical subject was more responsive to own score than to partner's score, but the partner's score was given some weight, in this case a negative weight—the higher the partner's score, the less desirable to the subject was the pair of outcomes. This indicates of course a tendency to use the partner's score as a CL.

The general effect of the CL is that one is dissatisfied unless own outcomes are as good as or better than those of the partner. This constitutes only one of the many ways in which people take account of other persons' outcomes. The important research of McClintock and his colleagues suggests that even in laboratory games there is considerable diversity in the forms of "account-taking." For example, in one laboratory study McClintock (1972) asked subjects to write down the reasons for their choices in the game. The principal answers they gave could be categorized as follows: (1) to try to get as many points as possible for myself, (2) to keep the lead, (3) to catch up with the other player, (4) to help the other player get more points, (5) to get as many points as possible for both of us, (6) to get the other player to play differently, (7) to try something new, (8) to learn something about the game or the other player, (9) for no precise reason, and (10) for miscellaneous reasons. In a later study McClintock asked subjects to indicate on each trial what outcome they preferred and, using the foregoing list, to indicate their reason for that preference. In both Belgian and American samples of subjects, 85% of the reasons fell in the first five categories. The variety of ways in which people take account of their own and others' outcomes is also indicated by research in Poland by Grzelak and his colleagues (Grzelak, Iwiński, & Radzicki, 1975; Radzicki, 1976). The analysis both of choices made in games and of rankings of pairs of outcomes (own and partner's) indicates that persons differ in the relative importance they attach to their own outcomes, to whether the partner is high or low, and to equal rather than unequal outcomes. In general the most common forms of pattern responsiveness in laboratory research have been found to be concern that one's outcomes be ahead of the partner (or at least not behind), concern that both outcomes be as high as possible (a kind of joint welfare concern), concern that the partner's outcomes be as high as possible (an altruistic concern), and concern that the two outcomes be as equal as possible (a justice or equity concern).

Within ongoing personal relationships, in contrast to temporary laboratory pairings of strangers, there has as yet been little investigation of pattern responsiveness. One interesting line of work has been reported recently by Walster, Walster, and Traupmann (1978). Each member of a heterosexual dyad is asked to rate, on a scale ranging from extremely positive to extremely negative, his or her own contributions to and outcomes from the relationship and the partner's contributions and outcomes. These ratings are entered into a formula that determines whether or not the member is receiving as much "profit" from the relationship (outcomes minus contributions) relative to his "investment" (contributions) as is the partner. The index derived from this formula presumably reflects the person's sense of being underbenefited, overbenefited, or equitably treated relative to the partner. Other measures of affective reactions to the comparison with the partner indicate that this presumption is generally correct. The research reported by Walster et al., based on some 500 undergraduates in casual or steady dating relationships, compared persons reporting themselves to be in equitable relationships with persons whose ratings indicate them to be either underbenefited or overbenefited. The persons in equitable relationships report (1) longer prior duration of the relationship, (2) greater expectations that the relationship will continue, and (3) greater intimacy in sexual relations with the partner. Furthermore, when followed up several months later, persons in the equitable relationships are more likely still to be going together. This research suggests that the members of heterosexual dyads make intradyadic comparisons of the rewards and costs of the interaction and that they place great importance upon being equal to their partners in enjoying the benefits the association makes possible. More generally (and more speculatively) these results probably make the important point that the development of voluntary personal relationships usually proceeds along lines of mutual rather than asymmetrical dependence. This mutuality affords equal bargaining power and a resulting rough equivalence in the allocation of rewards and of costs.

The Walster, Walster, and Traupmann study suggests that members of personal relationships are responsive to *differences* between their own outcomes and the partner's. Other evidence from ongoing dyads reveals another kind of responsiveness, in which the person shows concern that both own outcomes and the partner's outcomes be as high as possible. In other words the individual's evaluation of an event reflects some *summation* of its consequences for him/herself and for the partner. The relevant data are from a questionnaire study conducted at U.C.L.A. in 1978 by Steven Fleiner and myself. It follows the procedure outlined in chapter 2 for the example of cleaning the apartment. Ninety-six students rated their own satisfaction—dissatisfaction with common events occurring in their relationships with persons of the opposite sex. These ratings were made for two cases: Case I, in which the partner has no preferences about the possible events, and Case II, in which the partner has clear preferences. Case I permits us to estimate the person's own *given* outcomes, and Case II permits us to see how his evaluations are affected by the partner's outcomes.

For the example shown in Fig. 3.1, the question for Case I reads: "On a given evening, there are two movies you may go to: (1) a movie that *you* very much want to see and (2) a movie that you don't care about. [Your partner] has no preference about which movie to see." Ratings were made for four possible events: "1. You go together to the movie you want to see; 2. You go alone to the movie you want to see and [your partner] goes alone to the other movie; 3. You go alone to the other movie and [your partner] goes alone to the movie you want to see; 4. You go together to the other movie." The average ratings for the four events are shown in the left portion of Fig. 3.1. The components of the matrix, derived by the analysis of variance procedure, are listed below the matrix for Case I. Not surprisingly, there is a large BC component: The person has a strong interest in going to a movie *with* the partner, regardless of which movie

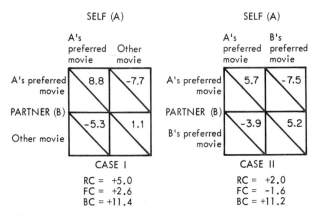

FIG. 3.1. Own outcomes for choice of movies when partner has no preference (Case I) and when partner has a preference (Case II).

they go to. However, the person is much more satisfied if they jointly attend his preferred movie (8.8) rather than the other one (1.1). This preference is reflected in both the RC and the FC terms, especially the former.

The question for Case II is similar except that it specifies that the partner prefers the "other" movie. The resulting ratings are shown in the right portion of Fig. 3.1. There is still a strong BC component, but the RC is weaker and the FC reversed, reflecting a modification of own outcomes to take account of the partner's preference. Thus whereas in Case I the person (A) wants the partner to go to A's preferred movie (to the extent of 2.6 units), in Case II the person wants the partner to go to the partner's preferred movie (to the extent of 1.6 units). The "responsiveness" to the partner's outcomes is most apparent in the lessened preference for going together to A's preferred movie over going together to the other movie. In Case I the difference is 8.8 versus 1.1, whereas in Case II it is 5.7 versus 5.2. Clearly the person's evaluation of the possible events in the situation reflects some compromise between his own movie preferences and those of the partner. The person gains some satisfaction from knowing that the partner is enjoying good outcomes and suffers some loss of satisfaction from knowing that the partner is attending the nonpreferred movie.

As long as the partner has no preference as between the two movies, the person evaluates the possible events primarily in terms of own direct (*given*) outcomes (Case I). Going together to one's preferred movie yields the greatest satisfaction. In Case II, when the partner has a preference, the person gives that preference some weight in assessing the alternatives. The result is a modification of the evaluative responses to the situation. Own preferences are partially suppressed, and the person is more desirous of going to the movie the partner prefers. This is of course a part of our everyday experience in relation to persons for whom we feel affection: "I want to do what will make you happy."

A second example of responsiveness to the partner's outcomes is shown in Fig. 3.2. The situation here is one of very low, perhaps minimal, interdependence. For Case I the question reads as follows: "You and [your partner] have decided to spend the evening quietly together, each reading a book. You have brought along two books to read, one that you like and one that you don't like." For the Case I example the partner has no preference: "Your partner has two different books to read, book X and book Y, which [your partner] likes equally well.'' For Case II the partner's preferences were indicated: ''Your partner has two different books to read, one that he/she likes and one that he/she doesn't like.'' The four possible events that the subjects rated consisted of all combinations of each person reading one book or the other.

In the absence of the partner's preference, this should be a simple situation of RC, the person's outcomes varying only with his/her own choice of books. This is found to be true for Case I. The only variance component in the person's outcomes is an RC of 13.0. The person is more satisfied by 13 units when reading the liked book than when reading the disliked one. Case II, in which the partner has reading preferences, provides a clear contrast. The person is now subject to FC, being 6.4 units more satisfied

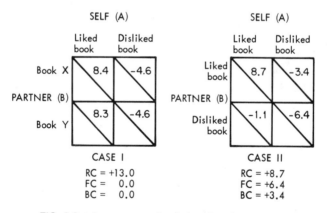

FIG. 3.2. Own outcomes for choice of reading materials when partner has no preference (Case I) and when partner has a preference (Case II).

when the partner reads the liked book than otherwise. The salient feature of the pattern is the 8.7 outcome, when both read their preferred book; presumably this reflects not only one's direct satisfaction with the preferred book but also the additional satisfaction gained from knowing that the partner is also engaged in what is for him/her an enjoyable activity.

The preceding examples show that members of young heterosexual couples evaluate events in terms of their combined consequences—that is, *both* own and partner's outcomes should be as high as possible. Although this may be the *typical* tendency, data Tim Patterson and I gathered in 1975 indicate that some members of these dyads may use other evaluative criteria. The sample of 100 dating couples first rated nine situations of the type described above. They then made further ratings in a procedure modeled after that of Wyer (1969) mentioned earlier. Each person rated how desirable he/she would find a series of 25 unspecified events to be, depending on the degrees of direct satisfaction that self and partner were experiencing. In other words the person rated the overall desirability of 25 pairs of own and partner's outcomes. Each person's desirability ratings were then correlated successively with (1) own outcomes, (2) partner's outcomes, (3) own outcomes plus partner's outcomes (simple summation), (4) own outcomes minus partner's outcomes, and (5) the absolute difference between own and partner's outcomes. We then simply noted which of the five correlations was largest for each respondent. The percentages of the 200 respondents for whom each of the correlations was largest are as follows: (1) 18%, (2) 5%, (3) 48%,

(4) 2%, and (5) 27%. These results are consistent with the preceding ones in indicating a general tendency to be responsive to the sum of own and partner's outcomes (48%). However, a sizable number are most responsive to own outcomes (18%), and an even greater number (27%) are concerned that the difference between the two outcomes not be too large. (The correlations with the absolute differences are uniformly negative, the small difference being more desirable than the large.)

To be emphasized here is the variety of forms that responsiveness to the pattern of outcomes may take. We must be concerned about the self-presentational biases possibly present in the data summarized above. However, by and large the results are consistent with our common experience in personal relationships, in which we are concerned not only about our own direct outcomes but also about those of the partner and about how the two compare. I now turn to a theoretical analysis of this phenomenon.

THE TRANSFORMATION OF INTERDEPENDENCE PATTERNS

In the preceding examples we see evidence of the modification of evaluative responses to various events in interaction. A person can respond, under certain conditions, only to the direct consequences of the event for the self. This is the way very young children respond, and it is the way adults respond when they are not aware of the consequences of the event for other people or when they believe it has no such consequences. However, with awareness of its consequences for others, a person can and does evaluate the event partially in relation to those consequences. This constitutes a transformation of the person's motivation. This transformation is elicited and shaped by the pattern properties of interdependence.

In our new book, *Interpersonal Relations* (1978), Thibaut and I develop a theory of this phenomenon of pattern responsiveness. A schematic outline of this theory is shown in Fig 3.3. We first make a distinction between the *given* and the *effective* matrix. The *given* matrix summarizes each person's direct outcomes as these are determined by his own and his partner's actions and without any account being taken of the effect of those actions on the partner's outcomes. In game research the *given* matrix is the set of payoffs specified for each person by the experimenter. In real life the *given* matrix is a set of outcomes provided to the person by external reward and incentive systems as these relate to his interests, needs, abilities, and the like. In the preceding examples, Fig. 3.1 and 3.2, the *given* matrix is defined by Case I in each instance and the *effective* matrix by Case II. As indicated in Fig. 3.3, each outcome in the *given* matrix is determined independently, simply as a function of the direct consequences of the action or actions and what these consequences are, in rewards and costs, for each individual.

The theory simply states that there is a process (called the "transformation process") in which the interdependent persons perceive certain properties of the *given* pattern and govern their behavior according to those properties (and not simply according to their

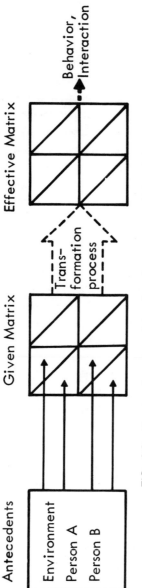

FIG. 3.3. The transformation of interdependence patterns. (Adapted from Kelley and Thibaut, 1978.)

own outcomes in the *given* matrix). They may, for example, act so as to maximize the joint or total outcomes in the *given* matrix. By adopting a criterion of this sort, they in effect act according to a different matrix. That is, they *transform* the *given* matrix into a different one, which is the *effective* one. It is the *effective* matrix that is directly linked to behavior.

This process can be illustrated with a pattern of MFC, as in Fig. 3.4. In a *given* matrix of MFC, neither person has a basis for action. That is, there is no RC. The person's actions do not affect his own outcomes, and there is no basis in those outcomes for choosing to do one thing or the other. (If this violates the reader's intuitions about this matrix, it is because the reader has a well-learned propensity to do what we are about to do—namely, transform the matrix in a manner that takes account of both persons' outcomes.) In Fig. 3.4 a transformation is made in which each person maximizes the total or joint outcome. That is, each person reacts to the sum of own and other's outcomes in each cell. With a mutual *max joint* criterion (transformation), the effective matrix provides each person with a basis for action and the result

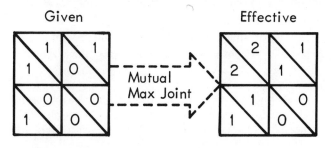

Given   Effective

Mutual
Max Joint

FIG. 3.4. *Max joint* transformation of MFC.

is an assured good outcome for both. Without this transformation, when each person would be attentive only to own outcomes in the *given* matrix, the outcome would be uncertain and not assured to be good. Thus, there is a benefit gained by both persons through the mutual *max joint* transformation.

The reader will recognize in this theory a partitioning of causes. The causes of interaction behavior are separated into (a) those that account for the *given* matrix and (b) those involved in the transformation process. As we apply this theory to the close personal relationship, our attention focuses particularly upon the stable personal factors that govern the transformations the person makes.

In *Interpersonal Relations* Thibaut and I make a functional analysis of the possible *origins* of transformation tendencies. We first ask whether or not there are any benefits to be gained by the person from transforming the *given* matrix. The answer to this question is sought by identifying all the major patterns of interdependence that might characterize the *given* matrix. These are the 20 or so major patterns identified by means of the component analysis described in chapter 2. Each such pattern is subjected to all the major transformations that have been identified empirically or that seem plausible intuitively or theoretically.[1] As described in the following, these include

---

[1]This statement should be qualified somewhat. We considered all the transformations that are rather simple and that apply to the entire pattern of interdependence. There are other important transformations to be identified and analyzed as to their functions. One example is provided by the conversion of FC to BC (Thibaut

(1) outcome transformations, (2) transpositional transformations, and (3) sequential transformations. We then ask whether or not, if one or both persons were to make each transformation and were to act according to it, they would be better off than if they had acted simply according to the rule of maximizing own outcomes in the *given* matrix. The analysis reveals

---

& Kelley, 1959, pp. 104–106). This requires the person exercising the power temporarily to suppress his responsiveness to his own outcomes (a temporary outcome transformation) and, through managing always to act after the partner does (a transpositional transformation), to ensure that the partner consistently experiences a certain contingent relation between behavior and consequences. A second example, of great importance to personal relationships, is provided by the process of "commitment": This term refers to many things, but in the interpersonal context it often represents a pledge, implicit or explicit, to suppress one's responsiveness to certain outcomes to be obtained outside the relationship. Thus the threat to relationship stability constituted by these external outcomes is reduced insofar as the person can manage not to "look at" or "think about" them. This may be seen as a transformational means of maintaining an artificially low Comparison Level for Alternatives (Thibaut & Kelley, 1959, pp. 100–101). Another transformation that encourages one's dependence on the partner is a special kind of *max own* transformation, in which those *given* outcomes controlled by the partner are supervalued. The preceding transformations are to be contrasted with others that serve to reduce one's dependence, which include the "bargaining" transformations of seeking and appreciating good alternatives and suppressing one's appreciation of rewards controlled by the partner. A third example is provided by the interpersonal concept of "tolerance." This often refers to accepting the partner's faults and idiosyncrasies. Tolerance is facilitated by selectively suppressing one's responsiveness to the FC or BC that the partner would otherwise exercise, for example by not responding to the costs produced by annoying mannerisms.

two benefits to be derived from transformations: (1) In some patterns actions based on certain transformations yield the persons better outcomes in the *given* matrix; (2) in some patterns certain transformations provide a basis for action (RC) where none exists in the *given* matrix. The latter would presumably provide the benefits of quick, conflict-free action in contrast to uncertain, time-wasting vacillation.

We have already seen for the MFC pattern (Fig. 3.4) that both of these benefits are provided by a particular *outcome transformation*, the mutual *max joint* transformation. Without the transformation neither person has a clear basis for action, and as a consequence the outcomes for the two persons are uncertain. With the mutual transformation each person has a basis in the *effective* matrix for choosing the action that, in the *given* matrix, helps the other person, and the resulting choices yield mutually good *given* outcomes.

The mutual *max joint* transformation provides a somewhat different benefit when made for the well-known Prisoner's Dilemma pattern in Fig. 3.5. Each person has a basis for choice in the *given* matrix, but

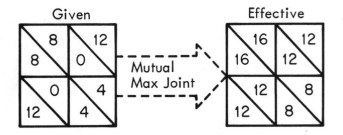

FIG. 3.5.   *Max joint* transformation of PDG.

inasmuch as this RC is discordant with the MFC component of the pattern, the choices made on the basis of the *given* matrix yield each person only 4 units of *given* satisfaction. With a mutual *max joint* transformation, the choice is shifted to the opposite actions (left column and upper row), and the choices converge on the cell that yields the better +8 outcomes in the *given* matrix. Thus, choices made according to a mutual *max joint* transformation yields better *given* outcomes than do choices made simply to maximize own outcomes in the *given* matrix.

These examples illustrate the potential benefits of one particular outcome transformation—the mutual *max joint* transformation. We also considered other outcome transformations, including (1) maximize other's outcomes, (2) maximize own relative outcomes (one's advantage relative to the other person), and (3) minimize the difference between own and other's outcomes. Each of these transformations yields benefits to one or both persons under certain conditions.

Another kind of transformation, the *transpositional transformation*, is produced by taking account of the microtemporal implications of the matrix. This transformation consists of the reconfiguration of the pattern of the matrix produced by one person's acting before the other one does. It is particularly appropriate when the pattern has an MBC component and reflects the benefits to be gained in certain cases by being the first to act (preemption) or in other cases by being the second to act (waiting and acting after the other person does). Fig. 3.6 shows the transpositional transformation produced for the pattern of correspondent MBC when Person B acts first. B's first

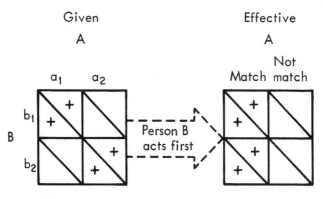

FIG. 3.6.   Transpositional transformation of CR−MBC
(Person B acts first).

action changes A's choices inasmuch as A then has, in effect, the choice of whether to match B's first choice or not to match it. A matching choice in this pattern will of course yield both persons good outcomes, and a not-match choice will yield both poor outcomes. Given the *effective* matrix produced by A's first choice, B then has a clear basis for choice and his probable action benefits both persons. This is a complicated way of showing that with correspondent MBC it is in both persons' interests to have a rule in which one person acts first and the other then acts appropriately. Here the unilateral transpositional transformation serves the common interest in the same way that the mutual *max joint* transformation serves the common interest with MFC.

The third kind of transformation takes account of the macrotemporal implications of the matrix. These are referred to as *sequential transformations* and are reflected in the common wisdom as turn-taking rules. An example is provided by the Threat Game in Fig.

3.7. In this pattern as *given*, Person B's RC leads him to choose b_1, and A's RC leads him to choose a_1. The result is satisfactory for A but not for B. B is likely to become dissatisfied with this state of affairs and to threaten to do b_2 (hence the name of the game). The obvious solution is for B to continue, on repeated occasions, with the b_1 choice while A alternates between a_1 and a_2. This constitutes one of many such sequential transformations for noncorrespondent patterns of this sort, and the result is an average value (per interaction occasion) of 3 units of satisfaction for each person. If either A or B might find it difficult to accept this solution and to forgo the opportunity of gaining 6 units each time, the matrix could be further transformed by invoking a *min diff* transformation, in which the difference between the two person's average outcomes is minimized. In a sense the problem is solved by A's being "fair" or "just" (minimizing the difference by his alternation) in exchange for B's being "loyal" (continuing with the b_1 choice that makes it possible for both to enjoy satisfaction from their relationship). In social psychological research this Threat Game has been the paradigmatic situation for Thibaut and Faucheux's investigation (1965) of the development of this tradeoff between justice and loyalty.

These examples illustrate the three kinds of transformation we have identified and suggests the mutual benefits they yield when made for certain patterns of interdependence. Thibaut and I argue that these theoretically identified benefits of transformations, which occur for *some* transformations applied to *some* patterns, provide the basis for the existence of transfor-

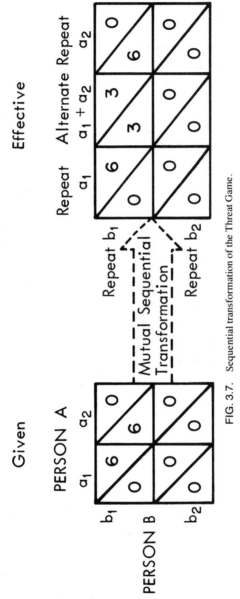

FIG. 3.7. Sequential transformation of the Threat Game.

mational tendencies. By virtue of their benefits such tendencies will have been learned, both in the history of social life and in the social development of the individual. They are taught to the individual as beneficial rules and norms (rules of considerateness, fairness, turn-taking, etc.), and this teaching is reinforced by the individual's experience in situations of interdependence. And by virtue of their functional value, through association with the benefits they provide, these transformations often become valued in and of themselves. They become internalized as values to be served without regard for the *given* consequences for the self. As they become autonomous of the *given* outcomes and made with regularity, the transformations become part of the interpersonal dispositions of the individual, as discussed in the next chapter.

This functional analysis of the possible origins of transformational tendencies is in part a theoretical statement of the origins of moral norms and values. However, it is also a theoretical statement of the origins of egoistic and immoral rules and practices. This can be illustrated by reference to asymmetric outcome transformations of the pattern known as Chicken, shown in Fig. 3.8. If Person A makes a *max rel* transformation (i.e., adopts the criterion of maximizing his advantage relative to B's outcomes), he acquires a clear RC basis for taking action a_2. If person B knows this, then the BC acting on him makes it desirable for him to take his b_1 option. This yields A his best outcome in the *given* matrix. Experience in situations of this sort will afford A a basis for learning to make the egoistic *max rel* trans-

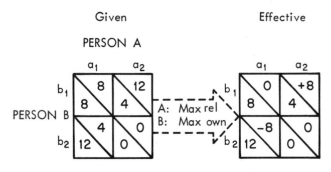

FIG. 3.8.   Asymmetric transformations of Chicken.

formation. Other similar cases can be constructed to provide a theoretical basis for the learning of such egoistic or immoral transformational tendencies. (Incidentally, from this sort of experience B will also learn something of importance, which is not to get into interdependence situations characterized by the Chicken pattern or at least not to do so with persons who are disposed to make *max rel* transformations, i.e., to be competitive.)

In general our analysis gives a theoretical view of how to get along successfully in interdependent social life. If we take our set of possible patterns of interdependence as representing the major variations in the basic problems existing in interpersonal relationships, then our analysis suggests the kinds of transformational rules people should learn in order to cope with those problems. The analysis shows that there are potential benefits to be derived from egoistic or antisocial transformations as well as from altruistic or prosocial ones. Thus we would expect the well-trained and fully adopted social individual to show a flexibility in the kind of transformations he/she adopts. One interesting result of the analysis is the absence of any indication that a person is ever better off being wholly altruistic (i.e., making a *max other* transformation) rather than being partially so (making the *max joint* transformation). The analysis suggests that well-adapted persons will always give some weight to their own outcomes.

An important result of the analysis is that the rules for optimal implementation of transformations involve double contingencies: The best transformation (in terms of *given* outcomes) depends on both (a) the nature of the interdependence and (b) the transformation the partner is making (or is prone to make). An example of the latter point is provided by the asymmetric outcome transformations of Chicken (Fig. 3.8). Person A benefits from adopting a tough, competitive stance (the *max rel* transformation) in this interaction with B, who merely maximizes his own *given* outcomes. However, if A were to make this same transformation against a different B, who was inclined also to be competitive and to make the same transformation, A would be likely to incur the poorest *given* outcomes in the relationship. Egoistic transformations such as *max rel* are to be adopted only with other persons inclined to pursue their interests as *given* or to make prosocial transformations. The other side of the coin is that Person B does badly in Chicken with his *max own* "transformation" when A follows a *max rel* criterion. Yet in interaction with a different A, who was inclined to make a *max joint* transformation, B's *max own* tendency would yield very good outcomes.

The same general point can be made by consideration of the PDG pattern. In Fig. 3.5 we saw the benefits each person gained from a mutual prosocial transformation. In the *effective* matrix, each one is led to make a choice that yields both 8 units of *given* outcomes. However, the story is different if one person makes a *max joint* transformation (as in Fig. 3.9), whereas the other makes a *max rel* transformation. The competitive person (A) benefits from his own a_2 choice whereas the cooperative person (B) suffers a loss from his b_1 choice. At least, B suffers poor *given* outcomes. If he is a true cooperator and has internalized the value of maximizing the joint welfare, then he may be satisfied with the 12 units of satisfaction indicated in the *effective* matrix and be able completely to set aside the poor outcomes suffered in the *given* matrix. However, we suspect that few people are able completely to set aside their reactions to the *given* outcomes. The point is that with a cooperatively disposed partner the *max joint* transformation permits B both to satisfy certain moral values and to get good *given* outcomes. In contrast,

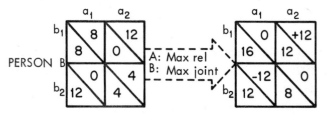

FIG. 3.9.   Asymmetric transformations of PDG.

with a competitively disposed partner, A's *max joint* transformation creates poor *given* outcomes and possibly an uncomfortable conflict between those outcomes and the outcomes in the *effective*, transformed matrix. I will return to this problem in chapter 5.

In general then the transformation a person should make depends on both the pattern of interdependence and the transformation the partner is willing and disposed to make. Therefore it is important for interdependent persons to understand each other's transformational tendencies. To the degree these are dispositional—that is, *stable* over time and *general* across situations—they are exceedingly important causal factors contributing to the resolution of interdependence problems and determining the course of the relationship. As I will emphasize in chapter 4, interdependent people are deeply concerned about such dispositions, both as they exist in their partners and in themselves.

Our analysis of the transformation process is theoretical and functionalist in nature. It specifies the transformations that the interdependent persons should learn (the learning of which they would benefit from). We do not go into the processes of this learning nor into the specific mediating processes that are learned. We are interested in the conditions, social and otherwise, that elicit various transformations. There is a sizeable body of literature in social psychology on this very topic, some of which is summarized in Kelley and Thibaut (1978). We do not deal with the specific psychological processes that make it possible for the person to set aside own immediate outcomes and become responsive to the total pattern. These are appropriate and important topics for developmental and motivational psychology. An excellent example of relevant research in this area is Walter Mischel's work (1973, 1974) on delay of gratification. His studies reveal some of the cognitive transformations of the stimuli associated with incentives—transformations that free the person from control by the immediately present temptations and enable delay of action in the interest of greater ultimate satisfaction.

To summarize this discussion of transformations of the *given* matrix: Interdependent persons show tendencies to transform the pattern of interdependence in which they find themselves (that is "given," or exists at the level of direct immediate consequences of specific behavior). In doing so they take account of the other person's outcomes as well as their own; that is, they are responsive to the total pattern of interdependence. Through this responsiveness they in effect transform the *given* matrix and act as if their interdependence were different from that specified by the *given* matrix. The origin of these tendencies is found, Thibaut and I propose, in the problems of interdependence themselves.

The theoretical analysis deals with transformations in general—for all patterns and for all types of other persons as partners. In the analysis of close personal relationships we must focus on certain of these transformations, primarily the prosocial ones, and (in chapter 4) look at some of the dispositional controls of transformations—at what are generally referred to as interpersonal attitudes, traits, and values. We must take account of certain implications of the theoretical analysis, particularly the double contingency rule:

that an individual's optimal transformation depends both on the nature of the interdependence and on the transformation the other person is making. We also find it necessary to identify the consistent patterning of transformations, suggestive of stable causes governing the transformation process. These transformations must be distinguished from tactical transformations made only briefly or intermittently for instrumental purposes, as in ingratiation or in setting the partner up for exploitation (the Con Game). We are especially interested in the particular kinds of stable causes that lie behind consistent transformations (traits, attitudes, values).

THE PERCEPTION OF TRANSFORMATIONS

According to Asch (1959) the individual's representation of "the situation that includes himself and others" contains "a reference to the fact that others also possess a corresponding view of the situation [p. 371]." This means of course that a person knows that the partner is aware of the person's outcomes. Therefore the person can perceive the partner as making transformations, that is, as being responsive in various ways to the person's outcomes.

Dissatisfaction with the partner's transformations is of course a common source of conflict. In lists of problems such as the one presented in chapter 2 (Table 2.1), complaints about the partner's failure to take account of one's own outcomes (lack of responsiveness) appear in a variety of contexts. In Category 3, Influence Attempts, the partner (the male, for example) is charged with always wanting the couple to do what he wants or with wanting her to do things his way without regard for her preferences. In Category 4, Failure to Give Appreciation, the partner fails to give praise or appreciation for what she does or is insensitive to her needs and feelings. In Category 11, Division of Responsibility, the partner is criticized for failing to do his share of the household chores or to make a fair contribution to the couple's finances. This category consists predominantly of dissatisfactions resulting from comparing own contributions to the relationship with those of the partner.

More systematic evidence about the perception of the partner's transformations is provided by the 1978 study conducted by Fleiner and myself described in the first part of this chapter. We had the respondents rate not only their own satisfaction with the four possible events in each episode (choice of movies, independent reading, etc.) but also the degree of satisfaction they estimated their partners would experience for each event. The results for the choice of movies are shown in Fig. 3.10. The ratings for self in the Case I and Case II matrices are the ones shown earlier in Fig. 3.1. It will be recalled that in Case I only the self has a preference between the two movies, whereas in Case II both self and partner have preferences but for different ones. Case III in Fig. 3.10. refers to the situation in which the partner prefers one of the movies, but the self is indifferent about them. The evaluations imputed to the partner for Case III are quite similar to those reported for the self in Case I: Going together to one's preferred movie is very desirable, but going together to the "other"

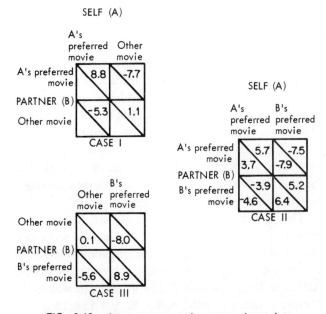

FIG. 3.10. Own outcomes and outcomes imputed to partner for three sets of preferences in choice of movies.

movie is close to neutral. Going alone to the preferred movie is rather negative, and going alone to the nonpreferred one is quite negative.

A comparison of Case II with Cases I and III shows the transformation made by the self and the transformation imputed to the partner. We have already seen that one's own outcomes are sharply modified to take account of the partner's preferences: Joint attendance of the preferred movie drops in attractiveness (from 8.8 to 5.7), and joint attendance of the nonpreferred one increases in attractiveness (from 1.1 to 5.2). The ratings imputed to the partner show the same effect *but to a lesser degree.* Going together to the preferred movie is perceived to decline in attractiveness (from 8.9 to 6.4), and going together to the nonpreferred one is perceived to increase (from 0.1 to 3.7). The difference between the reported and imputed transformations is seen most clearly in the Case II matrix, where the self favors joint attendance at one's preferred movie by only 0.5 units, whereas the partner is seen to favor joint attendance at their preferred movie by 2.7 points. (This difference is highly significant statistically.) It appears that one's partner is judged to be less responsive to one's own outcomes than one's self is to the partner's outcomes.

The pattern of results in Case II, which shows this perceived difference in transformation, was replicated for several other interdependent situations similar to the movie example. This effect had also been found earlier in Patterson and Kelley's 1975 sample of 100 dating couples. Furthermore, in the Patterson and Kelley study this bias in perception was also apparent in the direct rating procedure described earlier. Each person rated (1) how desirable he/she would find a series of unspecified events to be, depending on the degrees of direct satisfaction (a) self and (b) partner were experiencing. Each person similarly rated (2) how desirable the partner would find the series of events to be, depending on the degrees of direct satisfaction (c) the partner and (d) self were experiencing. The typical subject's own ratings of desirability correlated more closely with the partner's direct outcomes (relative to the correlation with own direct outcomes) than did the desirability ratings imputed to the partner. That is, $(r_{1b} - r_{1a})$ was greater on the average than $(r_{2d} - r_{2c})$. In short the partner was seen to be less affected by self's outcomes relative to his own than self is affected by partner's outcomes relative to self's own.

The preceding evidence indicates that in making *outcome* transformations the self is seen as taking more account of the partner than the partner takes of the self. A similar bias, but pertaining to the perception of sequential transformations (turn-taking), has recently been obtained by Ross and Sicoly (1978). Members of couples are asked to estimate the extent of their contributions to various activities (making breakfast, taking out the garbage, waiting for spouse). Each rating was made by a slash mark on a 150-mm line, the endpoints being labeled "primarily husband" and "primarily wife." When the portions of the line used to indicate each person's contribution were measured, the husband's and wife's portions consistently added up to more than 150 mm. In other words one or both persons overestimated the extent to which the self takes a "turn" at contributing to the welfare of the couple. Although this result is subject to a variety of interpretations, Ross provides evidence for the plausible idea that it reflects differential availability in memory of relevant events (Tversky & Kahneman, 1973). When the person makes a judgment of own versus partner's contributions, instances of the former more readily come to mind. A similar interpretation may be made of the Patterson and Kelley results in the foregoing. Each person may generally be more aware of instances in which he/she does things out of consideration for the partner's preference than of instances in which the partner reciprocates. The counter-self-interest (discordant

RC) makes such actions salient to the actor, but a desire to reflect a genuine "considerateness" in the action inhibits explicit expression of the overridden self-interest. (Such expression would threaten to define the action as an instrumental move to elicit a reciprocation of the benefit.) Thus the considerate act may often be salient for the self but go unnoticed by the partner.

In the next chapter we see what may be a further manifestation of this phenomenon when we examine evidence regarding attributional conflict. Persons are reported to give different explanations for their own actions than their partners give for the same actions. Two aspects of these differences are highly relevant here: Actors more often than their partners explain their negative behavior by their concern for the partner and by their consideration of the pair's mutual benefit. In contrast, partners more often explain negative behavior as being caused by lack of concern for the partner. Once again the results are open to a variety of plausible interpretations, but here is another indication that one's own responsiveness to the partner's welfare is more apparent than is the partner's responsiveness to one's own welfare.

Whether the individual's perceptions of the partner's transformations are accurate or inaccurate undoubtedly makes a difference in the course of the relationship. However, a more basic point for our present considerations is that such perceptions do exist. Through awareness of the partner's awareness of one's own outcomes, the self has a basis for imputing transformations to the partner. These imputations afford the possible basis for certain attributions to the partner, namely, attributions about the stable and general dispositional properties of the partner that lie behind the transformations. It is these attributions that I next consider.

The Attribution and Manifestation of Interpersonal Dispositions

4

The theme of this chapter can best be expressed by quoting from Fritz Heider's seminal work, *The Psychology of Interpersonal Relations (1958):*

> It is an important principle of common-sense psychology, as it is of scientific theory in general, that man grasps reality, and can predict and control it, by referring transient and variable behavior and events to relatively unchanging underlying conditions, the so-called dispositional properties of his world [p. 79].

For a concrete illustration, let us assume that a person, *p*, is confronted with an agreeable, happy experience, *x*. This is the raw material at a level close to the peripheral stimulus. The next step of interpretation may be: What is the immediate source of *x*? Is it chance? Am I the cause of it? Or is another person, *o*, the cause? If *o* is accepted as cause, the question of motive or intention may well arise. Did he do it in order to please me, or was the event only an accidental by-product of a different goal? Perhaps he was ordered to help me, perhaps he did it to put me under an obligation to him, or to relieve his conscience, or to please someone else. But if *p* perceives *o* as really wanting to please him, there are still deeper layers of interpretation possible. The need "*o* wants to please

p" may be caused by temporary goodwill in o; it may be "displaced love"; or it may come from a more permanent sentiment that o feels toward p. Finally, the underlying attitude itself may be traced to further sources. For example, p may feel that o's attitude toward him is a function of o's personality, that o is a kind person. Or, p, may feel that the sentiment stems from the compatibility in their natures, etc.

Underscoring the main points of this illustration, we note first, that man is usually not content simply to register the observables that surround him; he needs to refer them as far as possible to the invariances of his environment. Second, the underlying causes of events, especially the motives of other persons, are the invariances of the environment that are relevant to him; they give meaning to what he experiences and it is these meanings that are recorded in his life space, and are precipitated as the reality of the environment to which he then reacts [p. 81].

In this portion of my consideration of the personal relationship I begin with Heider's observation that the individual needs to refer observable events to invariant causes and that in the case of social behavior these "invariances" consist of other persons' motives, attitudes, and personality traits. I focus particularly on the dispositions of other persons that are expressed in the transformations they make. Of all the stable properties other persons possess, these *interpersonal* dispositions are the most important for close personal relationships. Such notions as respect, love, commitment, dominance, and competitiveness (to name a few) are conceivable only in relation to transformational phenomena. Their constellations of meaning may include specific events in the *given* matrix, but their essential meanings are both expressed and perceived in the ways that behavior becomes independent of the actor's direct consequences and responsive to the total pattern of interdependence.

Furthermore I argue that in personal relationships *the partners are interdependent with regard to these dispositions*. Each individual gains rewards and incurs costs as a function of the kinds of interpersonal propensities that he/she and the partner display in their interactions. In the theory of the personal relationship presented in chapter 5 it is necessary to take account of this interdependence that exists at the level of interpersonal dispositions and to analyze how it interacts with interdependence at the *given* level, the level of specific behaviors, and promotes patterns of transformation of the *given* matrix that determine the ultimate course of the relationship.

REFERENCES TO DISPOSITIONS AS SOURCES OF CONFLICT AND SATISFACTION

Before developing these theoretical points it is useful to consider evidence relating to personal dispositions and their importance in personal relationships. I emphasized in chapter 2 the unexpected frequency of personal dispositions in our respondents' statements of their problems and desires for change. Even though Cunningham, Stambul, and I emphasized to our 1973 interview subjects the necessity of giving examples of specific behavior, about 40% of the problems were described in nonspecific terms, often with reference to traits (passivity, impulsiveness, etc.). This tendency was even more frequent in the 1977 questionnaire study by Tiggle, Peters, and myself, in which about half the problems were stated in nonspecific terms. These results suggest the strong tendency to interpret specific negative behaviors in interaction in terms of stable, general causal properties of the actor. We see further facets of this tendency in a review of evidence on attributional conflict in the next section.

If closely related individuals often think of negative events by referring them to personal dispositions, they may do so even more for positive or satisfying experiences in their interaction. At least this is the implication of other results from the Tiggle, Peters, and Kelley study. We had the members of our couples (all married or cohabiting) list not only instances of how they wanted their partners to change (i.e., what they wanted them to *start* doing or *stop* doing) but also instances of what they wanted their partners to *continue* doing. These latter instances provide indications of the ways in which the partner is seen to provide one's self with rewarding experiences. It may first be noted that two-thirds of these items were described in nonspecific terms, with frequent mention of *stable* and *general* properties of the partner. The stable aspect is not surprising inasmuch as it is implied by the instruction: Something the person is desired "to continue" is by implication something he does on repeated occasions and that thus lends itself to description in stable terms. However, these descriptions are also cast in *general* terms, as general attitudes and general traits each of which can be manifested in a number of different ways. The most common indication of this generality is the use of the verb *to be* rather than verbs denoting action or "doing." Thus I want my partner to continue being affectionate, being honest, being religious, being ambitious, being a giving person, and so on. These "being" descriptions are common in the Tiggle, Peters, and Kelley data despite firm instructions to the subjects to list *specific* things they wanted the partner to continue *doing*.

We were interested in how what one desires one's partner to continue doing compares with what one desires the partner to start doing or stop doing. To obtain this comparison between sources of satisfaction and dissatisfaction we coded the "continue" items in the same categories used earlier for coding the problems arising in relationships. The problem categories were easily adapted to coding the desirable items by simply specifying the good behavior or properties (or the absence of the bad behavior) implied by each category. Thus in Table 4.1 the results in the "continue" column reflect desires for (1) open and good communication, (2) gentleness and even temper, (3) permitting person to make or participate in decisions, and the like. Several facts are apparent in Table 4.1. Far more of the "continue" items occur in Category 4 (giving appreciation, understanding, affection), and fewer occur in Categories 8 (being carefree, happy, and in a good mood) and 9 (careful, neat, and deliberate). The latter categories undoubtedly describe classes of behavior that when present are easily taken for granted but when absent are very distressing to the partner. Good moods, neatness, and self-control are generally expected of our close associates. Their presence goes unremarked, but their absence occasions problems for the relationship. In

TABLE 4.1

Classification of Problems and Satisfactions Reported by
Heterosexual Couples

Category	Percentages	
	Start/Stop Doing	Continue Doing
1. Inadequate & poor communication	7.3	5.5
2. Aggressive behavior & temper	3.8	0.2
3. Influence attempts, nagging, making decisions	3.6	3.9
4. Failure to give appreciation, understanding, affection	11.9	43.2
5. Independence, external involvements	0.1	3.5
6. Dependence, possessiveness	3.3	2.0
7. Passivity, lack of confidence, lack of ambition	16.6	14.4
8. Excessive worry, compulsivity, moodiness	8.6	3.9
9. Carelessness, sloppiness, impulsivity	17.3	1.5
10. Conflicting preferences about leisure time, where & how to live, etc.	8.3	8.8
11. Division & fulfillment of responsibility	6.4	7.9
12. Interference with partner's study, work, etc.	2.3	0.0
13. Inappropriate behavior in social situations	4.4	1.5
14. Attitudes & behavior toward parents	1.7	1.9
15. Attitudes & behavior toward friends	3.5	1.7

contrast, other types of behavior, as illustrated by
Category 7, are common sources both of dissatisfaction (passivity, lack of ambition) and of satisfaction
(self-confidence, ambition).

The most striking feature of Table 4.1 is the high
frequency of Category 4 items as things one desires

the partner to continue. The 43% in the category includes sex, affection, love, appreciation and reward, and understanding and support. Almost half of the items are of the last type: *understanding* (e.g., sensitivity, considerateness, tolerance) and *support* (e.g., encouragement and emotional support). These items show what we all know to be true of satisfying close heterosexual relationships, that at their core they involve a constellation of positive attitudes. These attitudes are general in their relevance, exercising a controlling influence over many specific behaviors. Although the members of these relationships can probably indicate some of the specific behaviors they want their partners to do, it is more important to them that the current positive attitudes continue. These attitudes have relevance not only for the specific problems the pair currently faces but also for various future circumstances, both known and unknown. It is only natural, then, for the members to express to us what they consider to be really important about their partners, namely, the (it is hoped) enduring positive attitudes and not particular current instances of specific behavior.

ATTRIBUTIONAL CONFLICT

Another set of evidence regarding the importance of stable general properties comes from investigations of attributional conflict, that is, disagreement between a person and the partner about the cause of the person's behavior. This type of conflict is illustrated by a special small set of problems in the Cunningham, Stambul, and Kelley study and in Tiggle, Peters, and

Kelley's data. These are cases in which the individual is annoyed that the partner draws unwarranted inferences from the individual's behavior. For example, one man was upset that his mate didn't understand his forgetfulness. She called him "irresponsible," or she said that he "intentionally forgot." In general, these are instances in which the partner explains behavior in a way that the actor cannot accept.

Starting with this sort of problem, we became interested in the phenomenon of attributional conflict. It has not yet been investigated as part of the content of open disputes within couples, but our studies suggest that it is probably an important theme in such disputes. In a first study, Bruce Orvis, Deborah Butler, and I (1976) asked the members of 41 young couples to describe instances of behavior for which the two of them had different explanations. One notable fact is the apparent ease with which the respondents were able to think of such examples, which suggests that disagreement about the causal interpretation of behavior is a common part of their experience. Furthermore, of the nearly 700 examples they provided, nearly all involved instances of negative or unpleasant behavior by one person. In other words (and not surprisingly) it is the unpleasant events within the relationship for which the two persons are likely to have different explanations.

Our procedure enabled a distinction to be made between (1) the explanation given by the actor for his/her own negative behavior and (2) the explanation given by the partner for the same behavior. The pattern of differences between actor and partner explanations is shown in Table 4.2. Partners, who are in

TABLE 4.2
Frequency of Use of Causes by Actors and Partners (Adapted
from Orvis, Kelley and Butler, 1976)

Causal Category	% of Actors	% of Partners	p-value
1. Circumstance/ environment	9.0	1.7	0.001
2. People/objects	8.1	4.8	0.02
3. Actor's state	8.1	3.2	0.001
4. Actor's preference/ belief	17.7	8.2	0.001
5. Actor's concern for partner and other people	7.4	2.5	0.001
6. Activity is desirable	15.8	6.9	0.001
7. Actor's characteristics	11.4	33.9	0.001
8. Actor's negative attitude toward partner	3.3	12.9	0.001
9. Activity has desirable indirect consequences	3.3	10.7	0.001
10. Actor's intention to influence partner	4.2	4.2	...
11. Partner is responsible	6.7	5.5	...
12. Activity is undesirable	3.5	1.9	...
13. Uncodeable	1.6	3.8	0.02

the position of complaining about the behavior, tend
to give explanations in terms of *personal* properties:
"Your bad behavior is caused (7) by your *personal
characteristics* [inability, poor judgment, irresponsi-
bility, selfishness] or (8) by your *attitudes* [lack of
concern for or negative attitude toward partner]."
There is also some tendency on the partner's part to
explain the behavior by reference to its indirect consequences (Category 9): "You did it to make a good
impression on other people or to project a certain
image." The actor's causal explanations seem to be of

two types: One type *excuses* the behavior, attributing it to (1) extenuating circumstances, (2) other people or objects, or (3) the actor's psychological or physical state. The other type of actor's explanation *justifies* the behavior, defining it as being (4) in conformity with norms ["I believed it was the right thing to do"] or as something the partner would accept (5) if its true intent were understood ["I did it because it was in your best interest"] or (6), if the desirability of the activity itself were appreciated ["Activity is desirable"]. In short, the partner's complaint about the actor's traits and attitudes is met by the actor's explanation that either excuses or justifies the behavior.

The foregoing view of the actor–partner attribution differences is nicely confirmed by a multidimensional scaling study recently completed by Passer, Michela, and myself (1978). Our purpose was to determine the underlying meaning that persons give to the various possible explanations for negative interpersonal behavior. Subjects were given all possible pairs of causes from a list of 13 causes adapted from the Orvis, Kelley, and Butler (1976) categories shown in Table 4.2. They judged the degree of similarity between each pair, and the resulting matrix of perceived differences was analyzed by the method of multidimensional scaling known as INDSCAL (Carroll & Chang, 1970). The interpretations of the resulting dimensions were based primarily on other ratings the subjects made using Semantic Differential bipolar scales to characterize the causes. In all cases the cause was associated with something one member of a marriage (the actor) had done that had displeased the spouse (the partner). For half of the subjects the causes were described as believed by the *actor* and for the other half of the subjects, as believed by the offended *partner*. These two sets of data yielded somewhat different solutions, as shown in Fig. 4.1 and 4.2, respectively.

One important dimension in both solutions is the attitude displayed toward the partner. Some causal explanations imply a positive attitude toward the partner and others imply a negative attitude. In both solutions this attitude dimension is anchored at the negative end by "Actor doesn't care for partner" and at the positive end by "Actor thought the behavior was in the partner's best interest." When the causes are understood to be believed by the *actor* (Fig. 4.1) the second differentiating dimension is that of *Intentional–Unintentional*. The most extreme causes at the Intentional end of the dimension are, "Actor wanted to change partner's behavior," "Actor thought the behavior was in partner's best interest," and "Actor believed it was the right thing to do." At the Unintentional end are located uncontrollable external and internal causes ("friends' pressure" and "actor's physical condition"). This dimension corresponds to the distinction noted earlier in the Orvis, Kelley, and Butler data between the actor's *justifying* and *excusing* explanations. The justifying explanations describe intentional behavior, done deliberately and for "good" reasons. The excusing explanations portray unintentional behavior, done because of external circumstances or temporary uncontrollable internal states. Apparently when our subjects in the multidimensional scaling study are told that the reason is believed by the actor, they attach a meaning to the explanation that

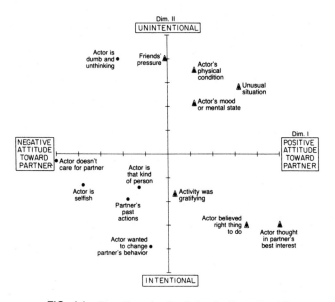

FIG. 4.1. Two-dimensional solution for "actor" condition. (From Passer, Kelley, and Michela, © 1978, by the American Psychological Association. Reprinted by permission.)

actors would be expected to—the meaning of justification or excuse.

In contrast, when the explanations are presented as believed by the partner (the offended spouse), the second dimension of meaning (shown in Fig. 4.2) is one that reflects the partner's attributional tendencies in the Orvis, Kelley, and Butler data, namely, explanation of behavior in terms of the actor's traits. The Trait end of the dimension is defined by "Actor is selfish" and "Actor is that kind of person." This property of the causal explanations, in contrast to nontrait explanations (temporary circumstances or states), is what our subjects, now identifying with the partner, take to be an important underlying dimension of meaning.

If we now relate the actor−partner differences in Table 4.2 to the two meaning graphs in Fig. 4.1 and 4.2, we see in very clear terms the general nature of the actor−partner attributional conflict. The types of explanations preferred by *actors* are indicated by triangles in Fig. 4.1 and those preferred by *partners* are indicated by circles in Fig. 4.2. In these two figures we locate each person's preferred type of explanation in the meaning space used by that person

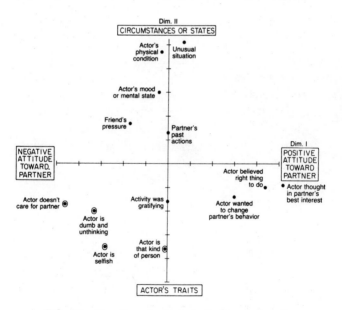

FIG. 4.2. Two-dimensional solution for "partner" condition. (From Passer, Kelley, and Michela, © 1978, by the American Psychological Association. Reprinted by permission.)

(as inferred from our two sets of similarity judgments). In Fig. 4.1 it can be seen that the actor's preferred explanations, whether excusing (unintentional) or justifying (intentional) in nature, imply for the most part a positive attitude toward the partner and certainly not a negative one. In Fig. 4.2 the partner's preferred explanations imply either a negative attitude or negative traits or both.

Further insight into the role of attributional conflict is provided by Bruce Orvis's recent dissertation research (1977). The method was derived from that of the Orvis, Kelley, and Butler study but involved greater standardization of the elicitation and response procedures. Data were obtained from 66 young heterosexual couples who had been dating for 1 year or living together for 6 months. Without going into the details, the results suggest that attributional disagreement is rather common, occurring occasionally even for positive events in the relationship. This is not surprising considering the great number of causal factors involved in any behavior, any one of which may be particularly salient to a person providing an explanation for it. However, Orvis's results also suggest that, as we might expect, attributional conflict is considerably more frequent for negative events.

Orvis wondered whether the pattern of actor—partner differences in attributions found in our original study is characteristic of differences in believed explanations or of differences in communicated explanations. His results on this point suggest that these actor—partner differences exist most clearly in what the two persons communicate to each other. In other words, what we've been seeing is primarily a scenario for open debate about the explanation for behavior. The occasion for this debate is suggested by correlation data from Orvis's study. Specifically, open attributional conflict occurs when there is conflict between the actor and the partner about how the actor's behavior is to be evaluated. It is on those occasions when the actor's explanation implies a more favorable evaluation of the behavior than does the partner's that attributional disagreement and communication about it are anticipated by the two persons. Finally, Orvis finds evidence consistent with the implication of Figs. 4.1 and 4.2, that the positive−negative attitude dimension is the principal axis along which the "negotiation" of attribution takes place. Variation in attitude as an explanation produces a very large shift in the evaluation of behavior.

We may step back from the details of our studies of attributional conflict and see in more general terms the nature of the phenomenon and its implications for our understanding of close personal relationships. The suggested scenario is as follows:

(1) A behavioral event occurs that is subject to differential evaluation, depending on its explanation. On the face of it the behavior has direct negative consequences for the partner. (2) In communication to the actor the partner tends to generalize from the event to a disposition of the actor—a negative attitude toward the partner or a negative trait. (3) On the other side the actor takes one of two positions: (a) it was merely a specific event, due to unstable or temporary causes, and it is not something to be generalized from; or (b) it reflects good general causes (e.g., my positive attitude toward you) and not bad ones.

In this scenario the actor and partner do not disagree about the relevance to their relationship of attributing specific behavior to stable dispositions. They simply differ in *whether or not* a particular event is to be so attributed and, if so, to *what* it is to be attributed. The actor's preferred attribution places the "negative" event within the context of positive attitudes and attempts to prevent its disrupting the relationship. The partner's favored attribution is less clear as to its function. Taken at face value the attribution to a stable negative causal factor does not bode well for the relationship. However, such attributions occur in apparently healthy relationships and are therefore probably not to be interpreted literally, as signs of despair. Aside from its expressive function the partner's attribution probably constitutes an attempt to influence the actor: a *sanction* that calls the actor's attention to how the behavior appears and that makes him/her feel ashamed of it and a *challenge* to prove otherwise in the future. Thus there is probably a double message: "Live up to your standards for yourself" (in general and in regard to our relationship), and "Show me it isn't so" (that you are inconsiderate, that you don't love me, etc.).

THE ROLE OF DISPOSITIONS
IN PERSONAL RELATIONSHIPS

We have seen that closely related persons make frequent references to each other's stable and general dispositions, both in commenting upon the sources of satisfaction and dissatisfaction in their relationship and in giving causal accounts of the behavioral events within it. As suggested in chapter 1, I believe this reflects an important aspect of the structure and functioning of the personal relationship. There are several points to be emphasized: First, as Heider (1958) suggests, the references to dispositions reflect each person's deep concern with the "invariances" upon which the relationship is based. Can the partner be counted upon? Is the partner genuinely considerate and thoughtful? Is the partner dependably capable and motivated? Given these concerns, specific behavior is scanned for its significance as to such underlying properties. It is attributed to attitudes, abilities, motives, and values.

Second, the partner's presentation or display of these properties has important affective consequences for the person. The display of positive properties is not merely reassuring about the future of the relationship but can also be a direct source of great satisfaction. The display of negative properties is not only a predictor of future problems but is directly punishing and cost-inducing. Third, one's own display of dispositions has consequences not only for the partner but for the self. Each one of us has preferences as to the attitudes and traits we reveal in our close relationships. We have standards or goals for the kinds of persons we are, the attitudes we have toward our partners, and the values we express in interaction with them. It is because of this fact that the partner's negative attribution of our behavior, if communicated and credible, can effectively constitute a sanction, making us feel ashamed, and a challenge to live up to our standards. Fourth, because the expression of dispositions has consequences both for the actor and for the partner, the individuals involved in personal relationships are interdependent with regard to these dispositions. Interdependence exists not only in the specific behaviors they enact but in the stable general properties they reveal themselves to have.

Finally, I would argue that the dispositions of greatest importance for personal relationships are those controlling the transformations the partners make—the *interpersonal* dispositions. This claim requires some explanation.

Dispositions and Transformations

A person will be concerned about a variety of stable properties of a partner in an enduring relationship. To the degree their outcomes in the *given* matrix are (presently) correspondent, reflecting similar needs and interests and complementary abilities and talents, each will be concerned about the stability of these factors that constitute the antecedents of the *given* matrix. Each will want to know that the outcome correspondence can be expected to continue because its antecedents are stable.

To the degree their outcomes in the *given* matrix are noncorrespondent,[1] each person will be concerned about what transformations the partner can be ex-

---

[1] An important qualification is that the outcomes must not be completely noncorrespondent. If there is perfect conflict of interest, there is no basis for mutually beneficial transformations. The reference here is to patterns with *some* noncorrespondence, usually referred to as "mixed-motive" patterns.

pected dependably to make. Is one's dependence warranted by the other's dependability? Can the partner be counted on to show sensitivity to one's outcomes and considerateness in taking account of them? Thus, given some conflict of interest, the important questions concern the partner's dispositions to respond to the *given* matrix in ways that are considerate of one's own outcomes. Furthermore, as actors in interpersonal relations, it is our own transformational tendencies in which we take special pride, for example, our dispositions to be loyal, brave, loving, etc. True, we may gain satisfaction from certain interpersonal skills relevant to specific outcomes and even from certain well-developed interpersonal tastes and needs, as in a "gourmet" approach to the rewards in the *given* matrix. However, the stable dispositions that generally give us greater satisfaction, as we find them in ourselves during close interpersonal encounters, relate to being able to transform the *given* matrix in certain ways. In short the most important dispositions are those relating to transformational tendencies. These *interpersonal* dispositions are highly important to us both as the qualities we seek in our partners for close relationships and as the qualities we seek to display in such relationships.

Interpersonal dispositions can be conceptualized as *rules* about transformations. Inasmuch as the transformations are themselves rules (i.e., rules about how to reconceptualize the *given* matrix), interpersonal dispositions are rules about rules or metarules. Examples are: "Always be considerate and thoughtful of your brothers and sisters," "Never let another person get the better of you," "Show respect for your elders,'' and, thanks to W. C. Fields, ''Never give a sucker an even break.'' The rules may be quite complex in specifying a variety of transformations. For example, ''showing respect'' implies outcome, transpositional, and sequential transformations that are favorable to the other person.

Common language includes a variety of concepts relating to interpersonal dispositions, and these vary greatly in the generality, over occasions and circumstances, in the applicability of the rules. Of least generality (and perhaps not qualifying as ''dispositions'') are such things as ''intentions'' and ''tactics'' (as in the ''tactics of ingratiation,'' Jones 1964). A person who desires to seduce another may make love-expressing transformations for the period of the seduction episode without these reflecting a more general rule (e.g., a more permanent attitude or commitment). Of greater generality are ''attitudes'' that are semistable orientations toward particular other persons. Attitudes of love, respect, loyalty, and so forth lead the individual consistently to make favorable transformations in relation to the particular partner but *not* more generally, in all other relationships. Such attitudes generate and are reflected in a series of intentions and the transformations appropriate to each intention. When governed by an attitude, the series of intentions has a coherence and meaning that it does not have otherwise. Of greater generality than attitudes are the phenomena referred to as ''values'' and ''traits.'' Interpersonal values, which are beliefs about the morally correct ways to treat people with whom one is interdependent, have a broad applicability over many other people, perhaps bounded only by ingroup – outgroup distinctions made by socializing agents. "Traits" are the most general dispositions. A person characterized by the trait of generosity will presumably make prosocial transformations in a wide variety of relationships and situations. His considerateness will not be unique to any given relationship.

Traits need not be as simple as the preceding example implies and need not be manifested in behavior that is consistent across situations. The "trait"-level rules governing transformations (and intentions and attitudes) may involve complex contingencies and therefore introduce a good deal of situational variability into behavior. For example, the Machiavellian person may place a contingency on W. C. Fields's rule, being very considerate of suckers who are judged likely upon being exploited to become effectively hostile. Similar contingencies may exist in the rules corresponding to attitudes: A person's attitude of love may be contingent, governed by the rule, "I'll love you as long as you love me." In such cases the variability will be patterned in relation to changing circumstances, but the underlying rule may be difficult to detect and the pattern may be hardly distinguishable from that produced by ad hoc, non-rule-governed, independent adjustments to successive situations. One of the unsolved problems of psychology is how to distinguish rule-governed variability in behavior, indicative of a stable "game plan" for life, from the variability that reflects an hour-by-hour coping with changing situational requirements.

THE ATTRIBUTION OF
INTERPERSONAL DISPOSITIONS

Interpersonal dispositions of the sorts just described are manifested in their essential, core meanings through transformations. They are both expressed and perceived in the ways in which behavior is independent of the actor's direct outcomes and is geared to the total pattern of interdependence. To speak of such things as love, courage, and considerateness is inconceivable without perceiving there to be a disjunction between behavioral choice and the chooser's *given* outcomes. Therefore the meaning of these concepts is based on a distinction in the minds of the participants that corresponds to the one represented here by the *given* matrix versus the transformation process.

This does not mean that interpersonal dispositions will be defined by the layman entirely in terms of transformational phenomena. Like other abstract concepts, they have a core meaning to which, through centuries of usage, more peripheral ideas have become linked. This can be illustrated for the interpersonal disposition ''love'' by reference to the research of Swensen (1972). He asked 300 people to list the ways they behaved, the things they said, and the ways they felt in relation to a loved person. He then selected almost 400 items from the responses, administered them in questionnaire form to a large sample of respondents, and factor-analyzed the results. The resulting factors, which summarize what Swensen's respondents mean by ''love,'' include both specific behavioral items (e.g., hugging, kissing, and

statements of affection) and transformational dispositions (tolerating the person's demands and negative
aspects; nonmaterial evidence of love: showing concern, providing encouragement and support). One of
the factors, material evidence of lóve, is defined by
specific behaviors that directly benefit the partner
(giving gifts, performing specific tasks), but there is
an implied sacrifice on the part of the actor, that is,
setting aside own interests in favor of the partner's
happiness. Self-disclosure of intimate facts, another
of the resulting factors, probably involves imputing
certain transformational tendencies to the partner: The
partner can be trusted not to exploit the intimate
information or to reject the discloser. Thus the partner
is seen as reciprocating concern for one's feelings and
tolerant of one's less pleasant aspects.

From Swensen's analysis we see that the meaning
of love includes both certain specific behaviors and
certain transformational tendencies. His data do not
enable us to test the present assertion that the core
meaning of the concept lies in the latter aspects. The
reader can appreciate the point by making a simple
thought experiment in which two persons are compared: one who hugs, kisses, and expresses affection
for the partner but who never shows concern or makes
sacrifices; and another who shows concern and makes
sacrifices but never hugs or kisses. We obviously find
it more natural to say that the latter expresses love
than that the former does. The latter expresses the
core meaning of love, whereas the former expresses
only the associated, peripheral meanings. In this
regard it may be noted that a majority of the items in
Rubin's Love Scale (1970) refer to transformational

tendencies such as concern for partner's welfare, tolerance of partner's faults, and interest in mutual self-disclosure. The remaining items express one's feelings when with or separated from the partner.

If transformations constitute the essential evidence of the dispositions relevant to personal relationships, then it follows that such relationships can develop and exist only if there is some problem in the *given* matrix to which transformations provide a solution. In chapter 5 I examine the relation between coordination and exchange problems and a variety of dispositions. We may presently consider the problems that arise from conflict of interest (noncorrespondence of outcomes) in the *given* matrix. With perfect correspondence of outcomes, there is no reason for prosocial transformations. That is to say, there is no way in which a person can make it clear he is acting out of regard for the partner's outcomes rather than his own. Thus there is no opportunity to display concern, willingness to sacrifice, and the like. The same is true, though perhaps with some qualification, for the display of negative transformational tendencies such as competitiveness, aggressiveness, and dominance. Again, these are most clearly seen when the actor enhances his own outcomes at the expense of the partner. However, they may be evidenced to some degree in situations of correspondent outcomes. Because we tend to assume that most people are somewhat concerned about their own outcomes (the thoroughgoing masochist being the rare exception), a person who acts to reduce both own and partner's outcomes will usually be seen as making a transformation in which the minimization of the latter is sought, that is, as acting out of spite.

A general point to be made here is that the dispositions that can be expressed depend on the *given* pattern of interdependence. The display of interpersonal "character" is made possible by but also limited by the *given* matrix. Without the interpersonal problems of coordination and conflict of interest, interpersonal dispositions would have no relevance for interaction. The specific dispositions "available" to the persons, both for display and for attribution, depend upon the specific patterns of their coordination and interest conflict problems. In most personal relationships the participants are probably little constrained in what dispositions they can display, because somewhere in the domain of activities over which they interact there are to be found the necessary patterns. However, some search for and selection of such patterns may be necessary, as when a man in love, desirous of making a telling sacrifice for his lady, goes out of his way to find an area in which their interests are noncorrespondent.

The attribution of transformations to a disposition requires that they be seen as caused by properties of the person that are to some degree stable and general in their operation (see the preceding discussion of dispositions). Existing research provides little evidence about such attributions. The most relevant studies have employed a very short time span, so we can hardly distinguish short-run tactical transformations from those reflecting more stable dispositions such as attitudes or traits. However, the general attributional bases for the kinds of dispositions we have been considering are clear: the *consistent display over time and circumstances of certain transformations*. For example, in a display of "considerateness" we would expect to see consistent outcome transformations in which the person gives weight to the partner's outcomes. Various transpositional transformations should also occur, including permitting the partner to go first in certain noncorrespondent situations but going first oneself in other correspondent situations so that the partner has merely to follow. Finally, there should be sequential transformations in which the person readily initiates and enters into turntaking sequences that permit the partner often to enjoy the most preferred outcomes.

The preceding comments emphasize the importance of consistency in the person's display of transformations. This does not imply that all instances are equally important in the eyes of the partner. There are often crucial events during which the person's transformations are taken as particularly revealing of dispositions. These are the occasions on which the partner is particularly dependent on the person, as in times of personal crisis or physical danger, and the person has strong personal interests counter to providing the needed help.

Of particular importance to the attribution of "stable attitudes toward the partner" will be a consistent pattern of transformations that occurs *uniquely* within the given relationship. This indicates the special nature of the relationship and provides the basis for its definition in terms of exclusivity. There is sometimes a desire, as in a love relationship, for both uniqueness and exclusivity—to feel that it is a type of relationship neither partner has ever had or ever will have with others. This desire is satisfied by the display of transformations made uniquely in relation to the particular partner: Each person is unusually self sacrificing or able bravely to face danger for the other. This is sometimes most easily demonstrated by a person who is generally rather slack morally, for example, the sadistic and self-indulgent male who, struck with love, becomes gentle and saintly in his relationship with the adored female.

As noted earlier, attitudes are to be distinguished from more general dispositions (values, traits), attitudes being unique to the partner. The more general dispositions are informative about the person who manifests them, but attitudes are also informative about the partner. Person A's attitude-regulated transformations indicate his perceptions of the partner, B, and thereby something about B. Person A's attitude of love toward B suggests that B is lovable. Person A's deferential attitude toward B indicates that at least in A's eyes B is worthy of respect. The significance to B of A's attitude and its derivative transformations is to be contrasted with the significance of similar transformations that reflect either generalized deference (a submissive personality) or tactical deference (ingratiation). If A's attitude implies properties of B in which B takes pride, then A's attitude will itself constitute a source of reward for B. The importance of such attitudes is shown in social—psychological research by the strong and well-replicated finding that one person's liking for another tends to elicit the latter's reciprocation of liking (Berscheid & Walster, 1978, pp. 39—45).

If A's attitude implies that B is characterized by certain interpersonal dispositions (e.g., proneness to be sensitive and considerate), then its expression will tend to facilitate B's making the appropriate transformations and interfere with B's making inappropriate ones. More generally, A's attitude may aid B in being the kind of person B wishes to be or may interfere with this pursuit. In these various ways, through validating or invalidating B's attempted dispositional displays and through facilitating or interfering with them, A's attitude expressions affect B's similar expressions. And of course B has a similar effect on A. We see here some of the workings of the interdependence between A and B in their display of interpersonal dispositions. In chapter 5 this interdependence becomes the focus of my analysis.

A Levels-of-Interdependence Model of the Personal Relationship

5

We now have the necessary concepts with which to elaborate a model of the personal relationship. Our preceding considerations imply that these relationships exist at two (or more) levels of interdependence. This chapter spells out this implication, gives illustrations of the model, and uses it to analyze the content and course of conflict.

In our model, shown in Fig. 5.1, the *given* pattern of outcome interdependence is basic to the relationship. It constitutes the foundation on which the rest of the relationship is built. It makes transformations necessary, and these in turn make possible the existence of interpersonal dispositions. The latter is indicated by the upward arrow in the figure. The transformation-controlling dispositions at the higher level are relevant only with respect to the interdependence problems existing at the lower, *given* level. Furthermore, these dispositions are manifested, that is, shown or expressed and perceived or attributed, only in terms of transformations of the *given* pattern.

The model gives a central role to the transformation process. Thus it emphasizes that the interdependent persons act not only out of consideration of the *given*

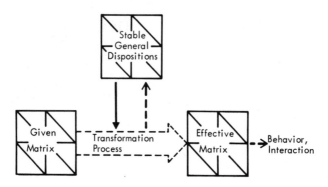

FIG. 5.1.   Model of the personal relationship.

matrix but also respond to its patterning, taking account of each other's outcomes. The ultimate course of the interaction is determined by the transformations as they generate the *effective* matrix.

The model reflects the assumption that the transformations are importantly controlled by certain stable, general dispositions of the persons—the interpersonal dispositions. (This, however, is not to deny that in personal relationships, as in all types of relationships, the transformations are occasionally generated by momentary intentions and tactics. An example of this is when, in the course of open conflict, a woman threatens to hurt her husband even if doing so means enduring considerable discomfort herself.)

As can be seen in Fig. 5.1, this model retains the partitioning of causes of behavior that the participants seem to make (cf. Fig. 1.1). The *given* matrix reflects the "direct consequences of specific behaviors," and the "stable general dispositions" in our model correspond to the "attitudes, traits, and values" in the earlier figure.

ILLUSTRATIONS OF THE MODEL

Before considering the technical details of the model, it will be useful to consider several *given* problems and the structures and processes to which they give rise.

Coordination Problems

Consider the brief but recurrent occasions of interdependence that arise when two cars, coming from opposite directions, meet on a two-lane road. The *given* pattern of interdependence is shown in Fig. 5.2, each person having the options of driving on the left or right side of the road. It is in both persons' interests for both to drive on either the left or the right, so the *given* pattern is one of correspondent MBC. This problem can be solved on an ad hoc basis on each encounter if one person will quickly and definitely steer to one side or the other and the second will observe that action and coordinate with it by steering

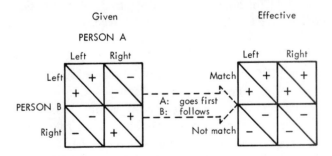

FIG. 5.2.   Interdependence and transposition for passing on two-lane road.

to the other side (also going to his *own* left or right just as the first person has gone to *his* left or right). This involves a transpositional transformation of the *given* matrix, the *effective* matrix shown in Fig. 5.2 being the result of A's going first and B's coordinating. It will be obvious to the reader that the two persons are interdependent in making these transformations: The *given* consequences for both are determined by whether both go first, one goes first and the other waits and coordinates, or both wait for the other to go first. Only certain combinations of the intentions to preempt or wait are satisfactory, just as in the *given* matrix only certain combinations of actions are satisfactory.

For *recurrent* situations of this sort it is possible for persons to adopt rules that govern their transformations on all occasions. Such rules yield great efficiency of action (eliminating the need for the individual to develop a specific intention on each encounter) and reduce the likelihood of incompatible intentions and resultant behavioral incoordination. For this particular situation the rule is always to use the right (or alternatively always to use the left) side of the road. This rule can be viewed as creating a transformation of the *given* matrix in which a preference for the right (or left) side is superimposed on the *given* MBC matrix—that is, RC is created for the one side. This rule affords an affective solution to the traffic coordination problem of passing. However, once again there are two equally useful rules, and drivers are interdependent in which one they adopt. It is a basic property of rules relating to coordination problems that there are two or more equally useful rules and that the adoption of one also involves a coordination problem. (See Lewis, 1969, on conventions.) The coordination problem is eliminated at the *given* level by the persons' following rules, but this in itself poses a coordination problem.

In the above example, adopting or following a rule constitutes a type of disposition. The rule indicates making a certain transformation on the *given* matrix. Doing so consistently for a given class of situations reflects a disposition of the person. Psychologically, this disposition probably consists of a complex of habits and preferences. The rule is followed more or less automatically, perhaps with some mild satisfaction at being on the correct side of the road and certainly with some discomfort when on the wrong side.

The driving example is rather distant from personal relationships, but it has its parallels in the coordination problems that highly interdependent persons encounter. From their desires to do things together (commonly referred to as "companionship") and from circumstances of limited space and facilities, there arise many problems of correspondent MBC. These coordination problems are solved in part by rules governing, for example, who will use the bathroom first or who will sleep on which side of the bed. They are also dealt with by interpersonal attitudes and traits. One person may have an attitude of superiority toward the partner and therefore feel it appropriate to be first or to select the side of bed. Or, as shown in Fig. 5.3, regularity in making the transpositional transformation in a certain way may stem from differences between the two persons in the trait of dominance–submission. The matrix in the upper portion of the figure shows the pattern of outcomes that A and B get from being dominant and submissive in their interaction. As with other coordination problems, good *given* outcomes are achieved only if a proper coordination of transformations is achieved. The outcomes in the disposition matrix reflect a different set of affective consequences for the two persons, relating to their preferences regarding their own and one another's transformation-regulating dispositions. Specifically, the simple pattern of outcomes in the disposition matrix in Fig. 5.3 reflects three facts (corresponding to its three components): (1) Person B prefers to act in a dominant manner in this relationship and A prefers to act submissively, (2) B prefers A to act submissively and A prefers B to act

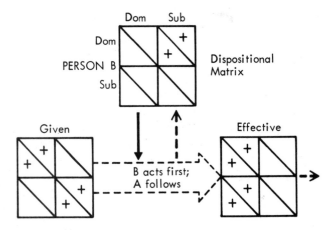

FIG. 5.3.   Facilitation of transpositional transformation by complementarity in dominance-submission.

in a dominant way, and (3) there is mutual facilitation in acting a certain way if the partner acts the opposite way (one person's submissiveness supports or validates the other's dominance, and vice versa). These traits are probably reflected in a variety of transformations made on *given* matrices, but for coordination problems B is prone to take the initiative and A, to wait, observe B's lead, and make appropriate adjustments. Thus the dispositional preferences shown in Fig. 5.3 facilitate coordination at the *given* level. The two persons are able both to satisfy their respective desires regarding dominance and submission and to achieve efficient coordination across a variety of situations.

Although the dominant−submissive pair is able efficiently to coordinate, other pairs (both preferring dominance or both preferring submission) are not. Experimental work indicates the validity of the point for ad hoc laboratory groups. Several studies summarized by Kelley and Thibaut (1969, p. 28) show that experimental coordination tasks are most effectively solved by pairs in which one person is more ascendant, dominant, or active than the other. Research on need complementarity in real-life heterosexual pairs may also point to the value of this type of dispositional asymmetry (cf. Turner, 1970, pp. 73−80). However, the dominant−submissive pairing may have deleterious consequences for other *given* interdependence patterns that most natural relationships will encompass. Accordingly, we are not surprised to find no clear relationship between this complementarity and, for example, overall marital adjustment (cf. Berscheid & Walster, 1978, pp. 78−81).

Although the two persons' dispositional preferences may not be such as to facilitate coordination,
the two may still obtain rewards at the dispositional
level. For example, both persons may prefer to sit
back and let the other take the lead. This set of transformational preferences will leave the coordination
problems to be dealt with by inefficient ad hoc
adjustments, but each person may find in this process
satisfaction of his/her preferences for passivity. If we
assume that the individual takes account of both sets
of consequences, then each will experience a disjunction between the *given* and the dispositional outcomes. The possible consequences of this are discussed later.

Exchange Problems

The Prisoner's Dilemma game is the prototype of
exchange problems. As described in chapter 2, this
pattern is composed of MFC with a BRC component
that is discordant for each person and of lesser
magnitude than the MFC. An example is shown in the
given matrix in Fig. 5.4. Each person is able to help
the other by "giving" but has a preference not to do
so, that is, to "keep." The benefits each can give the
other outweigh the costs to the giver of doing so. An
exchange of benefits occurs only if each person sets
aside the countervailing preferences. In the *given*
matrix the exchange always involves some intrapersonal conflict for each person. In any ongoing relationship this conflict sets the stage for one person or
the other to fail to give benefits *to* the partner while
receiving benefits *from* the partner.

The exchange problem can be solved on an ad hoc basis, through each person making the giving of benefit contingent upon receiving one. However, in complex relationships where giving occurs at different times and oftens consists of noncommensurable benefits, the ad hoc control of exchange is subject to breakdown. Person A's perception of the situation at any time as requiring giving or keeping may not agree with B's perception. A may give when B doesn't think he deserves to receive, which may give rise to questions in B's mind about A's costs in giving. Alternatively, A may keep when B feels his prior giving deserves reciprocation. Also, with fluctuations in A's circumstances he may not be able to act appropriately even when he perceives giving to be required. Strict reciprocity may be attainable only over a long time span. To insist on its fulfillment within a brief period (as with a very strict *min diff* or equity transformation) may make impossible what could be, over the long run, a very fruitful exchange.

At any given point in time, exchange is facilitated by mutual *max joint* (or *max other*) outcome transformations, as shown in Fig. 3.5. When this transformation occurs regularly, according to the rule of "always help the other," the exchange is promoted and the pair is spared the vicissitudes of the ad hoc process. The exchange problem is, then, a place where it is appropriate for people to display generosity, love, cooperativeness, and so forth. However, it is also a place for cynicism and competitiveness to flourish. The clever person can exploit others, his "success" being measured by how much he manages to receive relative to what he gives.

In exchange, as in coordination, people are interdependent in the transformation-regulating dispositions they manifest. With compatible dispositions, as when both have cooperative orientations to the relationship, each person is able to obtain reward at the dispositional level (through following his/her principles, expressing positive attitudes toward the partner, and being the recipient of similar expressions) and also to obtain satisfactory outcomes at the *given* level, derived from the specific concrete actions that constitute "giving" in the relationship.

With incompatible dispositions there exists a disjunction between the outcomes at the two levels. For example, in the interaction between cooperative and competitive persons, the outcome transformations are likely to be *max joint* and *max rel*, respectively, as shown in Fig. 5.4. The cooperative person (B in the example) "gives" as a means of promoting the joint welfare, but the competitive person (A in the example) "keeps" in order to maximize his relative advantage. At the *given* level, the result is unsatisfactory for the cooperative person. He is put in a conflict between expressing his preferred attitude and getting satisfactory *given* outcomes.

Research by Kelley and Stahelski (1970) and subsequent work by Miller and Holmes (1975) bear on this interaction in the PDG between persons with incompatible dispositions. The earlier investigation shows that most persons preferring to be cooperative will nevertheless shift to the "keep" choice when interacting with a competitive partner. The work of Miller and Holmes suggests that the intention behind this shift is not to become competitive in attitude but

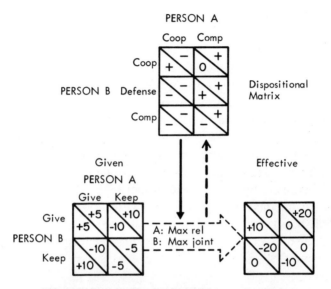

FIG. 5.4.   Interaction between cooperative and competitive persons in an exchange relationship.

rather to defend oneself against the other's actions. The dispositional matrix for this interaction may be represented as in Fig. 5.4. Person B has a preference to make cooperative transformations and will express this attitude unless the partner is competitive. In the latter case B reluctantly responds to the BC in the dispositional matrix and adopts a defensive attitude (e.g., minimizing own losses). Person A, the competitor, is shown as being subject only to RC in the dispositional matrix, preferring to make the *max rel* transformation regardless of what the partner does. Kelley and Stahelski (1970) also present evidence that in this situation the competitive A tends not to be aware of his partner's intentions and takes B to be competitively disposed, like himself. Furthermore, inasmuch as most of the cooperative persons A meets are like B, in taking the "competitive" action, A will develop the belief that most people are, like himself, competitive in their dispositions. Miller and Holmes's study (1975) adds the important qualification that A's faulty perception of B's disposition (mistaking the defensive attitude for a competitive one) occurs only if the *given* matrix provides no distinctive "defensive" response. Thus the errors in perception identified by Kelley and Stahelski result from the attributional ambiguity of the "keep" response in the PDG, it being the appropriate choice for a variety of transformations that serve quite different dispositions.

INTERPLAY BETWEEN THE GIVEN AND DISPOSITIONAL LEVELS

The preceding examples illustrate a number of aspects of the interplay between the two levels of the relationship and the processes to which they give rise. We see that although the two major types of interdependence problems are solvable on an ad hoc basis, for recurrent problems there are advantages in having general and stable rules that insure certain regularities in the transformations that are made. Adherence to these rules constitutes what we have referred to as interpersonal dispositions. The existence of the interdependence problems at the *given* level provides a basis for the development and existence of these dispositions. Persons interdependent at the *given* level may also be interdependent in their dispositions. Such interdependence exists when these dispositions are relevant to transformational solutions of the *given* interdependence and/or when interaction at the *given* level is interpreted and has reward – cost consequences at the dispositional level.

Once we make the distinction between the *given* and dispositional levels of interdependence, questions arise as to the exact nature of the interplay between the two levels. In answering these questions we incidentally gain some understanding of the bases of the pattern of interdependence that exists at the dispositional level.

To begin with, we may note the influence of the dispositional structure on the course of events at the *given* level. Some of the preceding examples show that the pattern of preferences at the dispositional level affects how the interaction goes. Certain patterns of outcomes in the dispositional matrix regularize coordination and reduce conflict. Other patterns have deleterious effects, causing one or both persons to experience higher *given* costs and/or lower *given* rewards than they might otherwise. In the latter case an individual will experience a disjunction between the outcomes of the two levels. For example, interacting with a competitive person in the PDG, a thoroughgoing cooperator will make consistent prosocial transformations in order to experience the satisfaction of fulfilling his dispositional ideals but will thereby experience the poorest *given* outcomes. (Unlike the defensive or contingent cooperator in Fig. 5.4, the thoroughgoing one persists in his cooperative attitude no matter what disposition the partner displays.)

My analysis assumes that persons can keep track of the consequences of interaction separately for the outcomes at the *given* and dispositional levels. Action occurs according to the *effective* matrix, which reflects both the *given* and disposition matrix, and ordinarily, when outcomes are adequate at both levels, the "accounting" of the interaction is in terms of the outcomes described by the *effective* matrix. However, because of their distinctive natures, the *given* and dispositional outcomes are readily separable— that is, they can rather easily be responded to (affectively) and taken account of separately. This disjunction occurs when the outcomes at one level are adequate and those at the other level are inadequate. The foregoing example illustrates the case of adequate dispositional outcomes but poor *given* ones. The experienced disjunction is reflected in a sense that the relationship is an *impractical* one. The opposite case, to be considered in the following, is that of adequate *given* outcomes but poor dispositional ones. The disjunction is reflected in a sense that the relationship is an *unfulfilling* one. These cases are to be distinguished from those in which both sets of outcomes are adequate or inadequate. In these cases the relationship is felt to be a good or bad one and the issue of practicality versus fulfillment never arises. In general, people tend to seek situations in which and partners with whom they can satisfy both the *given* and the dispositional needs. (The thoroughgoing cooperator will seek alternative partners so that he can meet his ideals without suffering concrete costs.) If unable to obtain satisfaction at both levels they often modify the dispositional preferences and become more contingent in the attitudes or orientations they adopt. (The contingent cooperator in Fig. 5.4 may have initially been a thoroughgoing cooperator but unable to find enough reciprocating partners to eliminate the punishing experience of being exploited.) Another adaptation to poor *given* outcomes is to suppress further their importance (beyond the suppression already required in making each transformation). The rewards at the dispositional level are exaggerated in significance, and life is lived for the satisfactions to be gained there, divorced from the practical considerations of the *given* level. In the extreme case poor *given* outcomes are taken as proof that the dispositional ideals are being fulfilled. "Pleasure" (satisfaction from *given* outcomes) becomes equated with "selfishness" and being exploited and deprived by others becomes a sign of one's success in adhering to high dispositional standards. These latter possibilities suggest that in certain extreme forms, transformation-regulating dispositions can become maladaptive. Although this volume has emphasized their adaptive value for the individual, there are important exceptions to this generalization.

The preceding paragraphs have dealt primarily with the control over coordination and exchange exercised by the persons' dispositions. It is also important to examine the upward effects in the model whereby the *given* matrix shapes and limits the expressions of dispositions and thus partly determines the pattern of interdependence at the dispositional level. The research by Miller and Holmes (1975) mentioned earlier illustrates the ambiguities involved in expressing dispositions through choices in the Prisoner's Dilemma

Game. In chapter 4 there was a brief discussion of the role that imperfect correspondence of outcomes plays in enabling both prosocial and antisocial attitudes to be expressed through transformations. This broad problem is discussed somewhat more fully in chapter 8 of Kelley and Thibaut (1978), but much analysis and research remain to be done on it.

The general point is that the *given* matrix determines how satisfactorily various dispositions can be expressed. It also determines the way in which the expression of a disposition by one person supports or interferes with the expression of a disposition by the other person. Through these influences the *given* matrix has an effect upon the pattern (RC, FC, and BC components) of the dispositional matrix. This effect can be understood by analogy to the determinants of the *given* matrix itself. Rewards and costs there are determined partly by the needs the persons bring to their relationship but also by the quality of the behavioral options they have as means of satisfying those needs and by the interference or facilitation between various combinations of behaviors. Similarly, the dispositional rewards and costs are determined partly by the dispositional needs or preferences the persons bring to their relationship but also by the quality of the means of expressing various dispositions and by the interference or facilitation between combinations of those means. The means and their interplay are determined by the *given* matrix. This will be explained more fully in the next section.

Because of the constraints the *given* matrix places upon the dispositional matrix, the *given* outcomes may be perfectly satisfactory but the dispositional ones inadequate. An example is provided by the competitive person who finds himself in a relationship characterized by high correspondence of outcomes. Deprived of a satisfactory way to *max rel* (for example), he may seek some other transformation that will enable a display of his ability to outdo the other. For example, he may suppress his own given outcomes and act to minimize the other person's. Or he may reconceptualize the interaction as one in which he manipulates the other's outcomes or behavior. (Recall from chapter 3 that some of McClintock's [1972] subjects gave as a reason for their choice, "to get the other player to play differently.") However, there are limitations to expressing a disposition in such unusual ways. Part of the value to the self of a display of competitiveness derives from the sense that the partner and observers of the relationship recognize its successful enactment. "Private" games afford less satisfaction than those in which there is a social response acknowledging that the desired impression has been made. This acknowledgment is shown in some cases by the partner's shift in attitude (as when he becomes deferent or even shifts to an apparent competitive stance). To elicit this "validation" of one's dispositional display, one must follow generally recognized rules regarding transformations (lest one's disposition be misunderstood), and the *given* matrix must permit the validating counterdisplay unambiguously to be made.

Probably the more customary response to poor dispositional outcomes is to find *given* matrices in which dispositions can be satisfactorily expressed. In part the mutual accommodation achieved within personal relationships reflects the identification of *given* domains of interdependence that permit mutually satisfactory expression of dispositions. If such domains are not discovered, an attempt may be made to find one or more alternative partners with whom the appropriate patterns of interdependence exist. A final possibility, most probable when the available range of *given* matrices is limited, is to modify one's dispositional preferences, adopting new attitudes and orientations that are better satisfied in the available settings.

PATTERNS OF INTERDEPENDENCE AT THE DISPOSITIONAL LEVEL

The reader may sense some problems in using the matrix concepts that are appropriate at the *given* level to analyze dispositional interdependence. The rows and columns in the *given* matrix represent actions or behaviors among which "choices" are made. How can one think of the person as "choosing" to be one way or another or to hold one attitude or another? I believe the difference here is one of degree and is not so great as to preclude adopting the same conceptual system for the two levels. In general the rows and columns of a matrix represent alternatives (in actions or in "being") that make a difference, separately or in combination, in the person's outcomes. To describe them as "choices" is to confuse structure with process, that is, the structure of the set of alternatives versus the particular process by which a certain alternative occurs. As noted in chapter 2, in our analysis of the *given* matrix Thibaut and I have not assumed that people always deliberately choose their actions. The occurrence of one or another of the alternative behaviors may reflect any one of a variety of psychological processes, including not only choice but also habituated behavior sequences, elicitation of unconditioned reflexes, and rule-governed social routines. No more at the dispositional level than at the *given* level is it to be assumed that the "enacted" alternative always represents deliberate choice and voluntary action. At the same time it does not seem unreasonable to assume that choice and voluntary control plays *some* role at the dispositional level. People do change their attitudes toward partners and vary the properties that they attempt to show themselves as possessing.

It also seems reasonable to use the concept of "outcome" at both levels, to refer to the rewards and costs associated with the specific behaviors at the *given* level on the one hand and with the transformation-regulating tendencies at the dispositional level on the other. The outcomes at the latter level simply refer to the satisfactions and dissatisfactions that people derive in personal relationships from having certain attitudes or feelings toward the partner, being a certain kind of person, and adhering to certain values.

The final question in the use of matrix concepts at the dispositional level is whether or not it makes sense to view the outcomes there as being interdependently controlled, that is, as involving MFC and MBC (as well as BRC) components. Descriptively this means simply that the person's dispositional outcomes depend not only on the dispositions he/she displays but also on the dispositions the partner effectively displays and/or on the combinations or pairings of dispositions they manage jointly to display. This volume is not the first to suggest the appropriateness of interdependence concepts for the description of the dispositional level of social interaction. The present conception of the dispositional matrix follows in its general outlines Robert Carson's proposal, in his book *Interaction Concepts of Personality* (1969), that the interdependence between people can be described at the level of generalized interpersonal styles.

As noted in the foregoing, the pattern of the dispositional matrix depends (1) on the dispositional needs or preferences the two persons bring to their interaction and (2) on the ways in which the *given* matrix makes possible the satisfaction of those needs or preferences.

Dispositional Preferences

To consider the first set of factors, we may note that the pattern tends to have a concordant BRC + MFC configuration (and therefore, a correspondence of outcomes) when there is consensus within the pair about how each person should be. Each one wants to be what the other wants him/her to be. This consensus need not require that the two display the *same* dispositions. In Fig. 5.3, both want B to be dominant and A to be submissive. Noncorrespondence stems from discordance between the RC and FC terms. An example is the male who will not (because of the absence of rewards or because of countervailing rewards) or cannot (because of the presence of costs) be as motivated or ambitious in life as the female wants him to be.

Behavior control exists when a person has contingent dispositional preferences, wanting to make certain transformations when the partner expresses one attitude but different transformations otherwise. This situation is illustrated by the contingent cooperator, B, in Fig. 5.4. If both persons are subject to BC, their preferences may be correspondent or noncorrespondent. For example, the two may prefer the same complementary combinations of activity−passivity for the pair, as in the left matrix of Fig. 5.5. Or, as shown in the right matrix of the same figure, one may prefer the complementary combinations (represented by a belief that they get along best when one is able to buoy up the other), whereas the other prefers that the two be similar in their general activity levels (believing that conflict is best avoided when they interact at a similar pace). The pattern of interdependence at the dispositional level can often be inferred from long-term changes in the nature of the interaction between the two persons. For example, the sharp mutual shift in attitudes often observed to be associated with

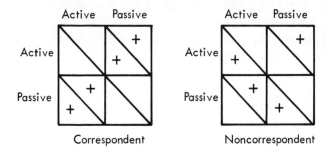

FIG. 5.5. Correspondent and noncorrespondent MBC patterns at the dispositional level.

disruption of marriage relations suggests an underlying correspondent MBC in a love—hate dispositional matrix. This pattern is consistent with a scenario in which one person's shift to hostility motivates a "coordinating" shift by the partner.

We saw earlier the implication of the theoretical analysis, expressed as the double contingency rule, that as far as the *given* outcomes are concerned, the individual's optimal transformation depends on both the pattern of interdependence and the transformation the other person is making. This suggests that if dispositional preferences are closely linked to *given* outcomes there will generally be a BC component in the dispositional matrix. One sign that a person has "internalized" a certain disposition (i.e., that its transformations are valued independently of the *given* outcomes) is its association with a strong RC term in the dispositional matrix. It represents a way the person wants to be regardless of the dispositions displayed by the partner. An FC component in the dispositional matrix reflects a preference that the partner will be a certain way in a noncontingent manner, that is, that the partner has internalized certain attitudes or traits relating to transformations (e.g., noncontingent love).

Effects of the *Given* Matrix

The second set of factors contributing to the pattern of the dispositional matrix derives from the particular *given* matrix with respect to which the dispositions are expressed. Certain *given* matrices facilitate the differential expression of certain traits or attitudes, whereas others interfere with such expression. (Some relevant evidence, from an unpublished study by Kelley, Jaffe, and Oliver, is summarized in Kelley and Thibaut, 1978, pp. 222–223.) For the former *given* matrices the variability in the outcomes associated with the related dispositions will be great: The preferred dispositions will be displayed in very clear and satisfying ways and the nonpreferred ones will be very much disfavored because of their unmistakableness. As a consequence the dispositional interdependence pattern will be a very clear one, with large components of all three types—BRC, MFC, and MBC. In contrast, *given* matrices that do not permit distinctive display of dispositions will tend to reduce the variability of the outcomes in the dispositional matrix. Neither great pleasure nor displeasure is derived from displaying a particular disposition.

The effects of the *given* matrix on the BC components of the dispositional matrix can be illustrated by a few examples. For *given* coordination problems (correspondent MBC), one person's preemption (first move) makes it difficult and unsatisfactory for the second one to display dominance but easy and satisfying for him/her to display submissiveness. In this simple way, by the structure of the *given* pattern, there is created an MBC pattern between dominance and submission at the dispositional level. (In the example in Fig. 5.3 this pattern is overlaid with complementary preferences for dominance and submission.) In other patterns, such as MFC, one person's harsh first action sets the stage for the other to resist the temptation to reciprocate and instead to show "tolerance" by returning a beneficent action. In certain patterns one outcome transformation tends to undercut and blur the meaning of a paired transformation. For example, let us assume in Case I of Fig. 5.6 that Person B, in a display of cooperative attitude, announces his intention to *max joint* and therefore his readiness to select b_1 as his action. Person A's transformational display of competitiveness is undercut, because in adopting the a_2 response indicated by his *max rel* transformation he also "cooperates" with B in maximizing the joint outcomes. This is in contrast

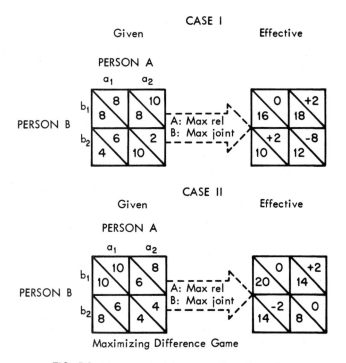

FIG. 5.6. Asymmetric outcome transformations of two *given* matrices.

to the Maximizing Difference Game (Case II of Fig. 5.6). A's *max rel* response (a_2) is clearly inconsistent with B's *max joint* intention and constitutes a more recognizable display of a competitive attitude. These examples show how certain *given* matrices permit the expression of one disposition to interfere with (Case I) or facilitate (Case II) the expression of another.

INTERACTION SCENARIOS

Chapter 2 briefly summarized the general types of interaction sequences associated with each property of interdependence. We may now consider how the interaction process is affected by transformations and their controlling dispositions. Transformations modify the process in a number of ways. Some of the important communication during interaction refers to transformations: Mutual transformations are proposed, one's own intention to reconceptualize the situation is stated, and values and norms are invoked to induce the partner to make certain transformations. When transformations are perceived to be controlled by known and dependable dispositions, the necessity for open communication and ad hoc negotiation is greatly reduced. In fact, for transformations to be effectively displayed as under dispositional control, it is often true that the less said the better. The husband must not ask the wife to do things for him if she is to be able to have her benevolent behavior appear spontaneous and disposition-generated (and if he is to enjoy it as such). We have all experienced the frustration of being asked to do something that we had intended out of good will to do anyway.

Any *given* matrix has within it the potential for a variety of plausible scenarios, as illustrated by the "cooperative exchange" versus "exploitation" versus "mutual standoff" scenarios for the Prisoner's Dilemma Game. The dispositional level of the relationship delimits the interaction by selecting among these possibilities. However, with the existence of the dispositional level, new aspects of the interaction become apparent. The communication includes references to interpersonal dispositions such as traits and attitudes. As suggested by the evidence on attributional conflict, such references often constitute attempts to use the dispositional outcomes to sanction a person for bad behavior. And of course references to dispositions may also constitute a powerful means of interpersonal reward when they provide explicit validation that the person is effectively being the kind of person he/she wishes to be.

Interaction can proceed at the *given* level, as in simple, casual conversation involving exchange of information, gossip, jokes, and so forth. Alternatively it can move to the dispositional level, becoming "personal" in the sense that events are taken as expressive of dispositions and as communications about dispositions. The shift to the dispositional level occurs in the "escalation" of conflict and competition, but it also occurs in the "escalation" of intimacy, trust, and love. As relationships become stable and secure there are sometimes complaints of being "taken for granted." An important aspect of this latter phenomenon is that the interaction proceeds mainly at the *given* level without attention to the expression of desired attitudes. This is most likely to be a problem when there exists a consensus at the dispositional level and little noncorrespondence of outcomes at the *given* level. Under these conditions few occasions arise spontaneously that, on the one hand, require or, on the other hand, enable the expression of dispositions. Attention to the dispositional level is most likely when conflict of interest exists, so that transformations become important and their controlling dispositions become issues. I now turn to a closer examination of conflict scenarios.

THE PROCESSES OF INTERPERSONAL CONFLICT

Conflict stems from noncorrespondence of outcomes at the *given* and dispositional levels. These different origins are reflected in the interaction scenario as expressions of unhappiness about the partner's specific behaviors (or the pair's joint actions) versus the partner's attitudes and traits (or the way the pair is "being"). Examples were provided in chapter 2 in summarizing the evidence from two surveys of couples' problems. Wanting different specific things to occur in their interaction or wanting different attitudes, the two can argue, quarrel, or, with cooler heads, negotiate which it shall be.

In these "discussions" (to use a neutral term), disagreements may be about the very outcomes themselves—about how various events should be evaluated. Just because the outcomes are one person's—

"belong" to one person, so to speak—does not mean that the other person may not have opinions about what they should be. Consequently the person makes assertions about the importance and value to himself of various things, these sometimes being honest statements and, sometimes, the kinds of exaggerations and distortions that give one a bargaining advantage. On the other side the partner, too, makes assertions about these matters on the basis of his own experience with the event at issue and his beliefs about the relevant properties of the partner. At the *given* level these are debates about how one should evaluate, for example, certain foods, certain movies, certain types of body contact, and so on. At the dispositional level the analogous debates concern the importance and desirability of expressing certain attitudes or traits in the relationship.

In attempting to agree about the future course of the interaction, the conflict "discussion" will include comments about exactly what behaviors and dispositions are to be enacted in the future. Also, a common topic of conflict concerns exactly what has been enacted in the past. Generally, the most important issues here concern the dispositional level. The question of what disposition has been expressed is also the most difficult one to answer. Because of the location of dispositions in the relationship, both *derivative from* the *given* matrix and *controlling of* transformations, a discussion about what disposition has been expressed potentially raises specific questions about every point and juncture in our model (Fig. 5.1): What are the true *given* outcomes? What transformations were made? What set of events constitutes the appropriate basis for drawing a generalization about transformation-controlling dispositions? Are certain events to be generalized from or are they to be treated as specific instances without relevance for dispositions?

The answers to these specific questions are interlinked, so one person may focus on one and the other person on another, with a resultant "cross-talk" and confusion. One scenario consists of the common attributional conflict in which the actor asserts the intrinsic desirability of the action and of its direct consequences for himself, but the partner attributes the action to something about the actor. To wit, in their explanations for one person's smoking marijuana or getting drunk, the actor says: "It's a release and I enjoy the times and activities while under the influence," whereas the partner says, "You're addicted and have no self-control." In this exchange the intrinsic value of the *given* outcomes is said to justify the behavior, but the intrinsic value is denied by the partner. The second, part of the partner's comment, "You have no self-control," moves the conflict beyond the *given* matrix to the level of personal dispositions.

Given the imbedding of the *given* matrix in the larger structure of the relationship, conflict does not remain long at the level of specific issues. This is perhaps the most important feature of the conflict process, that it escalates from the specific to the general, as shown in the common examples of attributional conflict. In the foregoing example, the absence of "self-control" clearly refers to a dispositional incapacity to make transformations in which one's own direct gratification is set aside. In the escalation process the set of instances relevant to the dispositional issue comes under debate. To support the allegation of dispositional inadequacies, the partner brings in other specific instances of behavior. The conflict becomes broadened to encompass a larger portion of the relationship.

Another aspect of the conflict concerns the transformations that have been made. Chapter 3 presented evidence that closely related persons tend to underestimate the transformations their partners make on their behalf. Specifically, each person feels that he/she takes more account of the partner's outcomes than the partner does of his/hers. The implication of this evidence is that the processes described above often take place against a background of inadequate appreciation of the degree of sensitivity and considerateness the partner has shown.

The relation between the *given* and the dispositional levels is intrinsically ambiguous. The members of personal relationships make the causal partitioning that corresponds to the two levels (Fig. 1.1), but they do not fully understand or analyze the distinction. The frequent lack of consensus about where the causes of behavior are located, revealed by research on attributional conflict, reflects disagreement not only about the evaluation of behavior but also about the level at which it has affective significance. When persons communicate their needs to one another there is often misunderstanding about the level at which satisfaction is desired. The ambiguity of the language of interpersonal needs is especially troublesome. As implied by Swensen's analysis of the meaning of love (1972, referred to in chapter 4), terms like *affection, considerateness, caring,* and *support* are used to refer both to specific behaviors in the *given* matrix and to general attitudes toward the partner.

Even when the partner's need is clearly understood in its dispositional aspects, ambiguity often exists as to what transformations one might make that will be (1) perceived as such and (2) attributed to the desired disposition. The problems here are illustrated by the husband who, when instructed by the marriage counselor to increase his rate of affectionate behavior, goes out of his way to wash his wife's car, but his wife fails to interpret this in the intended dispositional terms. Such good intentions go awry on the *expression* side when the husband misjudges the value of the act to the partner or assumes incorrectly that a concrete act of this nature is part of the connotative meaning the wife attaches to "affection." On the *attribution* side, the intended expression may fall short of its mark because the wife underestimates the costs to the husband of the particular action and therefore fails to detect that he has indeed "gone out of his way" for her.

From these ambiguities one sees the wisdom of the marriage counselor's search for the specific behaviors partners desire of each other. However, that approach deals only with the problem at the *given* level. To the degree persons are interdependent at the level of dispositions, their needs can be satisfied only by the manifestations of certain attitudes. To facilitate these satisfactions, the marriage counselor must of necessity delve into the complexities of self-presentation and attributions. The counselor must be attentive not only to the specific actions partners want but also to the signs they seek that the other person is responsive to their needs and is stably and generally so.

The Special Significance of Conflict

It is a commonplace that open interpersonal conflict usually arouses strong emotions. Consequently it often provides occasions for a test of the persons' transformational tendencies. To the observer, the person who is made angry or anxious by interpersonal conflict loses his "perspective," becoming less able to take account of the other person's and his own future outcomes and more exclusively focused on his own immediate outcomes. Own interests and impulses become strong, and the ordinary mechanisms that control them may not prove adequate. In everyday terms, the person "loses control of himself," "loses his temper," and "shows his true colors." The dropping out of certain transformational tendencies raises questions about the dispositions earlier attributed to the actor and suggests that the more stable tendencies may be less favorable to the partner. The stage is set on which a standard scenario of attributional conflict is played out. The partner interprets the shift in transformations as revealing true attitudes: "If you really loved me, you wouldn't act like this." The actor attributes the loss of control to the partner's provocation and his/her own emotional state.

The test of transformation tendencies that often occurs spontaneously during conflict is sometimes implicitly arranged by one or both of the partners. In families one child will sometimes provoke a sib to quarrel or fight in order to bring out the worst in the sib and thereby reveal to the parents what he/she "really" is. In a similar vein, Waller and Hill's (1951) analysis of the "lovers' quarrel" portrays it as a testing process that permits each person to demonstrate dependence on the relationship and that thereby often serves to strengthen it.

Conflict about Conflict

In view of its significance for the relationship and of its complexities and ambiguities, it is not surprising to find that the conflict process itself becomes a source of conflict. In examining any set of interpersonal problems, such as those classified in Table 2.1, one is struck with the frequency of behaviors related to conflict. Thus, the first three categories (Inadequate and poor communication; Aggressive behavior and temper; and Influence attempts, nagging, making decisions) are constituted primarily of instances of conflict about conflict behavior. The examples include failure to talk about problems, uncontrolled expression of anger, sulking and withdrawal during quarrels, and improper methods used to get partners to do what they don't want to do.

I wondered if this occurrence of "conflict about conflict" was unique to our samples of couples, who, in the contemporary university setting, have been exposed to much popular literature about communication, assertiveness, "how to fight" and so on. However, this seems not to be the case. Instances of conflict about conflict are common in studies of couples' problems, regardless of sample and date.

Even in Lewis Terman's classic study, published in 1938, many of the grievances that most clearly differentiated between happy and unhappy couples had to do with conflict behavior: Partner is argumentative, critical, nagging, complaining, quick tempered, oversensitive, and the like. It appears that the way the two persons fight and the interpretations they place on each other's conflict actions often afford further reasons for unhappiness.

In our own research, when we explored the reported problems further we found a number of indications that *part* of the conflict about conflict can be traced to differences between the *sexes* in their conflict styles. We first pursued this lead in a study (Kelley, et al., 1978) focused on sex differences in *comments* made during conflicts. Respondents of both sexes were presented with lists of comments that an unhappy member of the pair might make and that the partner might make in reply. They rated the likelihood that each comment would be made by each member of a heterosexual pair during an open conflict between them. A sample of 108 undergraduates made these ratings on a "stereotype" basis, that is, on the basis of their general beliefs about what men and women say in their fights. Another sample of subjects, consisting of 56 couples who had ongoing relationships, used the ratings to report what each of them would do or say if one of them was unhappy.

The main results are summarized in Table 5.1, which shows the comments (and actions, in parentheses) reported to be more common for each sex, both in the role of unhappy person and as the partner (source of the unhappiness). The stereotype and the report

TABLE 5.1

Reported Sex Differences in Comments Made during Conflict
(Adapted from Kelley, Cunningham, Grisham, Lefebvre,
Sink, and Yablon, 1978)

Unhappy female	Male partner
(Sulks)[a]	(Swears)[a]
(Cries)[a]	You won't convince me with your crying[a]
Do you realize how much you hurt me by acting this way?[a]	For once, put your emotions aside[a]
I feel so helpless because I just can't get through to you[b]	Face the situation logically[a]
This is really upsetting me. I can't handle it[b]	Don't get so excited[a]
Why do you always insist on getting your own way[b]	I don't want to talk about it now. I have too much else on my mind[a]
You never stop to consider my feelings[b]	What's the matter with you[b]
Let's just forget it[c]	Keep calm. It's not that important[b]

Unhappy male	Female partner
Face the situation logically[a]	(Sulks)[a]
(Swears)[a]	(Cries)[a]
As if I don't have enough problems, you have added this one[b]	You never stop to consider my feelings[a]
I think you should know how mad I am about this[b]	I don't think this is asking too much[b]
(Leaves)[c]	Please try to understand[c]

[a]Significant for both sets of data.
[b]Significant only for "stereotype" data.
[c]Significant only for "report" data.

155

data are rather similar, so I doubt that these data simply reflect sex role stereotypes. I am inclined to take the results as reflecting, at least in their general form, what are common behavioral differences between the sexes during conflict.

It can be noted that the behavior of each sex is pretty much the same whether that person is the unhappy one or the offending partner. The results suggest that the *female* of the pair, whether unhappy or offender, is more likely to cry and sulk, more likely to criticize the partner for lack of consideration of her feelings (e.g., "You never stop to consider my feelings"), and more likely to claim partner is insensitive to his effect on her (e.g., "Do you realize how much you hurt me?" "I feel so helpless because I can't get through to you").

The *male* of the pair, whether unhappy or offender, is more likely to show anger (e.g., he swears), more likely to reject the partner's tears (e.g., "You won't convince me with your crying"), more likely to call for a logical and less emotional approach to the problem (e.g., "Put your emotions aside," "Face the situation logically"), and more likely to give reasons for delaying the discussion (e.g., "I don't want to talk about it now. I have too much else on my mind"; "As if I don't have enough problems, you've added this one").

The foregoing view of sex differences in conflict behavior is quite well substantiated by results from a second study—a questionnaire study of 105 young couples, by Crawford, Kelley, Platz, and Fogel (1977). Members of these couples were given a list of items that described a variety of psychological situations in the relationship and a variety of conflict behaviors. The female and male separately judged which person each item was more characteristic of. These judgments were factor-analyzed, and factor scores were computed for each respondent for each of the seven factors.

The major results are shown in Fig. 5.7. This bar graph shows the degree to which the typical female (solid line) and typical male (broken line) judges each situation and/or behavior to be more characteristic of the female member of the pair (to the right) or more characteristic of the male member of the pair (to the left). (Some of the factors were defined only by situational items; others, only by conflict behavior items; and still others, by both.)

The graph shows that respondents of both sexes agree that the female is more dependent and vulnerable. (This situational difference is not, however, associated with any differences in conflict behavior, contrary to what the interdependence analysis in chapter 2 would lead us to expect.) Both sexes also agree that during conflict the female gives more stress to communication about the problem and about feelings. They also agree that the female tends to feel greater concern for the partner and, during conflict, is more likely to charge the partner with failure to reciprocate her concern for him.

The males more often describe themselves as having a self-interest linked to some external task and, during conflict, as being more likely to accuse the partner of interference with practical matters. (This reminds us of the comments from the earlier study: "I have other things on my mind"; "As if I don't have

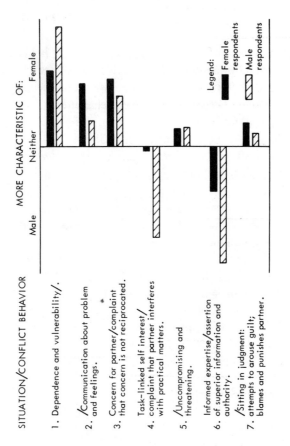

FIG. 5.7. Sex differences in psychological situations and conflict behavior. (Adapted from Crawford, Kelley, Platz, and Fogel, 1977.)

enough problems, you have to add this one.'') The male of the pair is also described as being in a position of informed expertise and, during conflict, as more often asserting his superior information and authority. Again, this is primarily the way males describe their own situations and behaviors. There is no evidence of sex differences in the two patterns of conflict behavior identified as "uncompromising and threatening" and "sitting in judgment."

Our results reveal the different approaches to the resolution of conflict that members of heterosexual couples are likely to adopt. Undoubtedly these differences themselves often contribute to further conflict. In general the two studies portray an interaction scenario between a conflict-avoidant person (the male) and a partner (the female) who is frustrated by the avoidance and asks that the problem and its associated feelings be faced.

A basic issue about conflict, then, is whether it will be dealt with explicitly or will be left at an implicit level. In its everyday functioning the personal relationship proceeds implicitly, with a give-and-take that is governed by informal rules and routines and with occasional verbal cues to facilitate coordination. Many specific conflicts of interest are worked out implicitly with merely a communication of pleasure and displeasure that affords a basis for adjustment and counteradjustment of behavior. This implicitness is often a sign that the transformational process is functioning successfully, the persons being sufficiently attentive to one another's interests that explicit discussion of them is unnecessary. It is not always obvious when it becomes necessary for problems to be dealt with explicitly. Our results suggests that in heterosexual couples it is more often the woman who first feels this necessity. Her call for an explicit expression of feelings and discussion of problems is apparently justified by her assertion that the transformation process has broken down on the male's side. He is no longer sufficiently sensitive or considerate and fails to reciprocate her attitude of concern. The male's counterassertion of his practical responsibilities outside the relationship serves as a justification for setting the problem aside but also perhaps as an excuse for what the spouse regards as lack of considerateness.[1]

A second issue about conflict suggested by our data is the familiar one of whether or not specific negative events are to be generalized from—that is, escalated

---

[1]John Thibaut makes the important observation that these results on sex differences in conflict suggest that the interdependence between the man and woman in our typical couple is that of the Threat Game, as shown in Fig. 3.7. The man is usually the one who controls the allocation of rewards within the relationship (Person A in Fig. 3.7) and the woman is usually the one (Person B) who is dependent on A's fairness. If A is unfair, B either accepts it or demands justice, using the threat of taking the b_2 action to back up the demand. One typical scenario for this pattern is consistent with our results on sex differences. Person A is too exploitative and B asks that the problem (of the unjust allocation) be discussed. It is in A's interest to avoid the discussion in order not to bring the matter to a head and to continue the exploitation. This strategy tends to work, at least in the short run, because B's exercise of the threat action (b_2) has such extreme negative consequences for the relationship that she is loath to take it. If forced to deal with the issue, A may try to justify his own superior outcomes by reference to his "important outside responsibilities" which are borne on behalf of the pair.

to the dispositional level. In relation to the specific attitudinal area of *concern*, the female is more likely to raise the general issue. In the data obtained by Crawford et al., both sexes agree that the female is generally more concerned about the feelings and needs of the partner and, during conflict, more likely to refer to the concern and support she has given the partner and to complain about the partner's inattentiveness and lack of consideration. Incidentally, we might guess that she takes the male's avoidance of explicit problem discussion as another indication of his poor attitude toward her.

This result is reminiscent of the conclusion from laboratory game research that females are somewhat more moralistic in their orientation to interpersonal relations. In his review of sex differences observed in gaming and bargaining studies, Terhune (1970) concluded that whereas women are more likely than men to seek a compromise and accommodation when faced with a conflict of interest, if this tendency is exploited by their partners they tend to respond with greater vindictiveness and retaliation. This is suggestive of a moralistic outlook in which a cooperative orientation to the interdependence is regarded as a "good" one and alternative orientations as "bad." In contrast, male subjects seem to take a more pragmatic approach to these games, doing their best to win and being willing without apparent qualms to exploit a partner's cooperativeness. However, if the partner's resistance to being exploited makes it a practical necessity, they are willing to become cooperative. In short males seem to have a strategic and flexible orientation to interdependence games, at least in the laboratory, whereas female subjects seem more prone to become ego-involved and to attach personal and moral meaning to the interaction. With reference to our model, the males remain closer to the *given* level, making transformations largely for tactical reasons and on a temporary basis. The females, in contrast, move to the dispositional level with their personal interpretations of the interaction. They tend in a sense to treat the laboratory dyad as if it were a personal relationship.

There is considerable uncertainty about the status of the foregoing sex differences, and they may be somewhat overstated in the preceding paragraph. However, there seems little doubt that these contrasting orientations do occur in personal relationships and that they add a special dimension to the conflict process. The contrast is between one person who is prone to take things personally, that is, to interpret them in terms of attitudes toward the partner, and a second person who judges the events more in terms of their direct consequences and the practical aspects of coping with noncorrespondent outcomes in the *given* matrix. One has little difficulty imagining the confusion and complexities of interaction between two such people and the special frustrations that their different orientations to conflict provide one another.

Concluding Remarks 6

The levels-of-interdependence model of the personal relationship is an attempt to take account of what I see to be the key properties of personal interaction. These are, briefly, interdependence, mutual responsiveness to one another's outcomes, and attribution of behavior to stable dispositions. From a consideration of these three phenomena I have developed a view of the personal relationship the central feature of which is interdependence in two types of consequences. Interaction proceeds simultaneously at two different levels, yielding both the direct and concrete outcomes described in the *given* matrix and the symbolic and abstract outcomes described in the dispositional matrix. Interdependence exists with respect to both types of outcomes—that is, both are controlled to a considerable degree by the partner and by the pair jointly. In an ideal relationship both types of outcomes are satisfactory, but in other cases the participants experience their relationship as impractical (unsatisfactory *given* outcomes) or unfulfilling (unsatisfactory dispositional outcomes).

Not all interpersonal relationships involve a great deal of interdependence at the dispositional level—

interdependence in attitudes and dispositions. A "personal" relationship can be defined as one in which the interdependence at that level reaches a certain criterion level. This definition is consistent with what is implied in common usage by references to a "personal friend," "becoming personal," or "taking it personally."

The model goes beyond the distinction between two levels of interdependence and attempts to describe the dynamic interrelations between them. The two levels do not represent simply two types of needs that jointly determine interaction and that are satisfied or frustrated during its course. On the one hand, the dispositional level represents a set of factors that are *derivative from* the conflicts and dilemmas at the *given* level, having their origins (in the development of both the individual and the relationship) in those conflicts and dilemmas. On the other hand, once "in place," the dispositional factors are *controlling of* how the problems of the *given* level are solved. Because this control is recognized by the participants, they interpret interaction events partly in terms of underlying dispositions.

The assumption here is not merely that the more abstract dispositional properties of the relationship are expressed through the concrete events at the *given* level. They are expressed in the particular ways (and patterns of ways) in which behavior departs from what is indicated by the *given* outcomes. In the present terminology, the dispositions are expressed through *transformations* of the *given* matrix. This important point is easily misinterpreted. There are other dispositions that act directly to determine the outcomes at the *given* level. These include the needs and abilities that underlie the response repertoires and direct outcomes specified in the *given* matrix. The present analysis identifies a distinctive set of *interpersonal* dispositions for special attention. These are the dispositions that have special relevance for social interaction and that serve the important function of loosening the causal linkage between the direct, concrete consequences summarized by the *given* matrix and interaction behavior. These interpersonal dispositions correspond to the attitudes and traits to which the participants refer in describing their interaction and from which they derive the pleasant and unpleasant consequences that constitute their higher-level interdependence. This is not to say that all the nuances of meaning in the participants' dispositional references (e.g., references to love, concern, dominance, competitiveness) are captured by transformations on the *given* outcomes but rather that the essential and irreducible core meanings are.

From this theoretical perspective, the study of the personal relationship must focus upon the participants' perceptions of each other's traits and attitudes. Analysis must be made of the processes corresponding to both the upward and downward arrows in the model (Fig. 5.1). The first consist of *attribution* processes that begin with perceptions of the *given* matrix and transformations made on it, proceed through a stage of organizing patterns of real or perceived transformations, and culminate in the formation of dispositional concepts. It is important to note that not only other-attributions are made here but also self-attributions, the personal relationship being the site in which a person learns much about his/her own interpersonal tendencies. The second consist of *expression* processes that begin with desires to be a certain kind of person or to hold certain attitudes toward the partner and proceed to use the perceived *given* outcomes to generate patterns of transformations believed to create the intended impression. In these processes each person is both expresser of own preferred dispositions and supporter or inhibitor of the partner's expressions.

This brief description of the central perceptual, conceptual, and expressive processes, though highly abstract and simplified, suggests some of the complexities of the phenomena involved. The possible sources of error in perception and inference are many. There may well be a background level of egocentric bias in the process, as suggested by the evidence on perception of own versus partner's transformations and of the causes for own versus partner's behavior. Against this background there are undoubtedly many major errors of attribution (underestimates of the partner's positive attitudes, misperception of the partner's needs relating to own dispositions, misinterpretations of the causes of own reactions to the partner) and failures of expression (inadequate clarity in displaying own costs and therefore the transformations being made; overreliance on concrete behaviors associated with the dispositional concepts at the expense of attention to consistent patterning of relevant transformations).

As the model emphasizes, interaction occurs in a context of thought. Thoughts about each other guide the participants in their actions and dispositional expressions. Moreover, action and expression are perceived by the participants to be guided by thought. Events are interpreted as reflecting intentions and attitudes. Yet thought is not always (or even usually) decisive in the control of behavior. Nor is it always perceived to be decisive. The perception of the causation of behavior is undoubtedly subject to enough error that there often develops a disparity between the two—between the true degree of thoughtful control of behavior and the perceived degree. A common disparity is when the latter is greater than the former, behavior being "overinterpreted" as to intentions and attitudes. A severe imbalance of this sort is undoubtedly destructive of a relationship, with every specific negative event occasioning an escalation to the dispositional level. However, according to the present view the general answer to this problem does not lie in cutting off references to intentions and attitudes and focusing exclusively on the interchange at the level of specific behavior and concrete rewards. To do so deprives the participants of some of the major satisfactions potentially available to them in the personal relationship. In some cases of serious disturbance a "decapitated" relationship, with the dispositional level removed, may be better than the one that exists when the participants are permitted to continue to "rely heavily upon a cognitive—motivational model of behavior" (as Weiss, Hops, & Patterson, 1973, put it). However, the possible costs of this restriction of the relationship must be kept in mind, and questions must be raised about the desirability of its continuation. For relationships that have a potential for restoration to a healthy state superior to what the participants are likely to find with other partners, the answer to current difficulties must lie in improving rather than removing the processes that make possible dispositional interdependence.

The scientific analysis of the attributional and presentational process central to our model will occupy us for some considerable time. The necessary evidence will be very difficult to assemble, involving as it must both the detailed and comprehensive longitudinal description of behavior and subjective accounts of feelings and beliefs that are obtained both in real-time, concurrently with behavior, and retrospectively. The difficulties of our analysis are of course reflections of similar difficulties the participants have in the accurate expression and attribution of traits and attitudes. That fact is the basis for the special fascinations of research on personal relationships. Our research procedures are similar, in some basic ways, to the participants' expression and attributional processes. In the thorough study of a personal relationship, we inevitably enter into a personal relationship with its members. As we try to give an account of the events in the relationship and the bases for their actions and attributions, we inevitably cover some of the same ground they do. Therefore our research procedures must be subjected to the same kind of careful analysis that we make of their internal procedures. Some complex interpersonal problems, bearing on the investigator's relation to the personal dyad, must be solved, for example, relating to our influence on the relationship, the systematic differences between outsiders' and insiders' perspectives, and direct involvement of the dyad in the research procedure (Kelley, 1977). With proper research procedures the student of the personal relationship has the fascinating prospect of gaining understanding of the private and shared worlds of its members. The unavoidable consequence of human social life is a realization of the essentially private and subjective nature of our experience of the world, coupled with a strong wish to break out of that privacy and establish contact with another mind. Personal relationships hold out to their members the possibility, though perhaps rarely realized in full, of establishing such contact. (Here there come to mind images of Asch's "mutually relevant fields" and Lewin's "overlapping life spaces.") The members of the best personal relationships are able to evolve a sense that they genuinely share world views and that each one is understood in the way that he/she understands himself/herself. In our study of personal relationships we have the challenging opportunity of identifying the barriers to such understanding and, in the best of our relationships with close pairs, of being allowed to enter their very consensus itself.

References

Aldous, J. Family interaction patterns. *Annual Review of Sociology*, 1977, *3*, 105–135.

Asch, S. E. A perspective on social psychology. In S. Koch (Ed.), *Psychology: A study of a science. Volume 3. Formulations of the person and the social context.* New York: McGraw-Hill, 1959.

Back, K. W. Influence through social communication. *Journal of Abnormal and Social Psychology*, 1951, *46*, 9–23.

Berscheid, E., & Walster, E. H. *Interpersonal attraction* (2nd ed.). Reading, Mass.: Addison-Wesley, 1978.

Blood, R. O., Jr., & Wolfe, D. M. *Husbands and wives: The dynamics of married living.* Glencoe, Ill.: Free Press, 1960.

Carroll, J. D., & Chang, J. J. Analysis of individual differences in multidimensional scaling via an N-way generalization of "Eckart-Young" decomposition. *Psychometrika*, 1970, *35*, 283–319.

Carson, R. C. *Interaction concepts of personality.* Chicago: Aldine, 1969.

Cartwright, D., & Zander, A. *Group dynamics* (3rd ed.). New York: Harper & Row, 1968.

Crawford, L. Y., Kelley, H. H., Platz, J. B., & Fogel, P. W. *Variations in conflict behavior within close heterosexual relationships.* Unpublished manuscript, University of California, Los Angeles, 1977.

DeBurger, J. E. Marital problems, help-seeking, and emotional orientation as revealed in help-request letters. *Journal of*

Marriage and the Family, 1967, *29*, 712–721.

Deutsch, M. An experimental study of the effects of cooperation and competition upon group process. *Human Relations*, 1949, *2*, 199–232.

Goode, W. J. *After divorce*. Glencoe, Ill.: Free Press, 1956.

Grzelak, J. L., Iwiński, T. B., & Radzicki, J. J. Motivational components of utility. Fifth Conference on Subjective Probability, Utility and Decision Making, Darmstadt, 1975.

Heider, F. *The psychology of interpersonal relations*. New York: Wiley, 1958.

Hill, C. T., Rubin, Z., & Peplau, L. A. Breakups before marriage: The end of 103 affairs. *Journal of Social Issues*, 1976, *32*, 147–168.

Jones, E. E. *Ingratiation: A social psychological analysis*. New York: Appleton-Century-Crofts, 1964.

Kelley, H. H. An application of attribution theory to research methodology for close relationships. In G. Levinger & H. Raush (Eds.), *Close relationships: Perspectives on the meaning of intimacy*. Amherst: University of Massachusetts Press, 1977.

Kelley, H. H., Cunningham, J. D., Grisham, J. A., Lefebvre, L. M., Sink, C. R., & Yablon, G. Sex differences in comments made during conflict within close heterosexual pairs. *Sex Roles*, 1978, *4*, 473–492.

Kelley, H. H., & Stahelski, A. J. The social interaction basis of cooperators' and competitors' beliefs about others. *Journal of Personality and Social Psychology*, 1970, *16*, 66–91.

Kelley, H. H., & Thibaut, J. W. Group problem solving. In G. Lindzey & E. Aronson (Eds.), *The handbook of social psychology* (2nd ed., Vol. 4). Reading, Mass.: Addison-Wesley, 1969.

Kelley, H. H., & Thibaut, J. W. *Interpersonal relations: A theory of interdependence*. New York: Wiley-Interscience, 1978.

Levinger, G. Sources of marital dissatisfaction among applicants for divorce. *American Journal of Orthopsychiatry, 1966, 36*, 803–807.

Levinger, G. A social psychological perspective on marital dissolution. *Journal of Social Issues*, 1976, *32*, No. 1, 21–47.

Lewin, K. *Resolving social conflicts*. New York: Harper, 1948.

Lewis, D. K. *Convention: A philosophical study.* Cambridge, Mass.: Harvard University Press, 1969.

McClintock, C. G. Game behavior and social motivation in interpersonal settings. In C. G. McClintock (Ed.), *Experimental social psychology.* New York: Holt, Rinehart, & Winston, 1972.

McClintock, C. G., & McNeel, S. P. Reward and score feedback as determinants of cooperative and competitive game behavior. *Journal of Personality and Social Psychology,* 1966, *4,* 606–613.

Miller, D. T., & Holmes, J. G. The role of situational restrictiveness and self-fulfilling prophecies: A theoretical and empirical extension of Kelley and Stahelski's Triangle Hypothesis. *Journal of Personality and Social Psychology.* 1975, *31,* 661–673.

Mischel, W. Toward a cognitive learning reconceptualization of personality. *Psychological Review,* 1973, *80,* 252–283.

Mischel, W. Processes in delay of gratification. In L. Berkowitz (Ed.), *Advances in experimental social psychology* (Vol. 7). New York: Academic Press, 1974.

Orden, S. R., & Bradburn, N. M. Dimensions of marriage happiness. *American Journal of Sociology,* 1968, *73,* 715–731.

Orvis, B. R. *The bases, nature, and affective significance of attributional conflict in young couples.* Doctoral dissertation, University of California, Los Angeles, 1977.

Orvis, B. R., Kelley, H. H., & Butler, D. Attributional conflict in young couples. In J. H. Harvey, W. J. Ickes, & R. E. Kidd (Eds.), *New directions in attribution research* (Vol. 1). Hillsdale, N.J.: Lawrence Erlbaum Associates, 1976.

Passer, M. W., Kelley, H. H., & Michela, J. L. Multidimensional scaling of the causes for negative interpersonal behavior. *Journal of Personality and Social Psychology,* 1978, *36,* 951–962.

Peplau, L. A. *Power in dating couples.* Unpublished manuscript, University of California, Los Angeles, 1977.

Radzicki, J. Technique of conjoint measurement of subjective value of own and other's gains. *Polish Psychological Bulletin,* 1976, *7,* 179–186.

Ross, M., & Sicoly, F. *Egocentric biases in recall and attribu-*

tion. Unpublished manuscript, University of Waterloo, 1978.

Rubin, Z. Measurement of romantic love. *Journal of Personality and Social Psychology*, 1970, *16*, 265–273.

Scanzoni, J. Social exchange and behavioral interdependence. In R. L. Burgess & T. L. Huston (Eds.), *Social exchange and developing relationships*. New York: Academic Press, 1978.

Sears, R. R. A theoretical framework for personality and social behavior. *American Psychologist*, 1951, *6*, 476–483.

Stambul, H. Braiker *Stages of courtships: The development of premarital relationships*. Doctoral dissertation, University of California, Los Angeles, 1975.

Steiner, I. D. *Group process and productivity*. New York: Academic Press, 1972.

Swensen, C. H. The behavior of love. In H. A. Otto (Ed.), *Love today: A new exploration*. New York: Association Press, 1972.

Terhune, K. W. The effects of personality in cooperation and conflict. In P. Swingle (Ed.), *The structure of conflict*. New York: Academic Press, 1970.

Terman, L. M. *Psychological factors in marital happiness*. New York: McGraw-Hill, 1938.

Thibaut, J. W., & Faucheux, C. The development of contractual norms in a bargaining situation under two types of stress. *Journal of Experimental Social Psychology*, 1965, *1*, 89–102.

Thibaut, J. W., & Kelley, H. H. *The social psychology of groups*. New York: Wiley, 1959.

Turner, R. H. *Family interaction*. New York: Wiley, 1970.

Tversky, A., & Kahneman, D. Availability: A heuristic for judging frequency and probability. *Cognitive Psychology*, 1973, *5*, 207–232.

Waller, W., & Hill, R. *The family: A dynamic interpretation*. New York: Dryden, 1951.

Walster, E., Walster, G. W., & Traupmann, J. Equity and premarital sex. *Journal of Personality and Social Psychology*, 1978, *36*, 82–92.

Weiss, R. L., Hops, H., & Patterson, G. R. A framework for conceptualizing marital conflict: A technology for altering it, some data for evaluating it. In L. A. Hamerlynck, L. C. Handy, & E. J. Mash (Eds.), *Behavior change: Methodology, concepts and practice.* Champaign, Ill.: Research Press, 1973.

White, G. L. *Inequality of emotional involvement, power, and jealousy in romantic couples.* Unpublished manuscript, University of Maryland, 1977.

Wish, M. Deutsch, M., & Kaplan, S. J. Perceived dimensions of interpersonal relations. *Journal of Personality and Social Psychology,* 1976, *33,* 409−420.

Wyer, R. S. Prediction of behavior in two-person games. *Journal of Personality and Social Psychology,* 1969, *13,* 222−238.

Zander, A., & Wolfe, D. Administrative rewards and coordination among committee members. *Administrative Science Quarterly,* 1964, *9,* 50−69.

Index